A Victorian Jou. Snowdonia, Caernarfon and Pwllheli

Snowdonia and the Llyn Peninsula are, in my view, unrivalled in terms of historical interest, delightful coastal resorts and scenic grandeur. Victorians who could afford the train fare and the time were of similar mind and made their way from England's dirty, grimy cities to this haven of fresh air, dramatic scenery and tranquillity.

On arrival, they needed to know what to see and where to go and guide-books were available to help them make the most of their stay.

This booklet combines text from a guide to North Wales, written in the late 1890s, with photographs from the same period.

It is remarkably detailed and includes chapters on how to get there and what to see on the way (with particular emphasis on Chester); the history of the area; walks; excursions to places of interest; climbing Snowdon; the Ffestiniog and Snowdon Mountain Railways and much more.

The original book, reproduced here, is over one hundred years old and not in the best condition. As a consequence, there are some marks, dark patches and other blemishes in this booklet. Also, the print is quite faint, so I've darkened the pages a little to ensure that the text is legible.

The photographs and illustrations within the body of the text are from the original guide-book. They were poor quality when first printed and still are. Those at the end of the book are from glass, 'magic lantern' projection slides dating from the 1880s to the 1920s and are much sharper and clearer.

The text and photographs complement each other and enable us to travel back in time to this historically important and stunningly beautiful corner of Wales. I hope you enjoy the journey.

Andrew Gill

CROMLECH NEAR CRICCIETH

PWLLHELI, CRICCIETH, FFESTINIOG, CARNARVON, SNOWDON, Etc.

Approaches to the District.

PWLLHELI, Criccieth, and Portmadoc are on the Cambrian line, and can be approached by way of Barmouth, by the Great Western *viâ* Bala and Ffestiniog, or by the London and North Western *viâ* Chester to Llandudno Junction (*refreshment rooms*), and thence *viâ* Bettws-y-Coed, Blaenau Ffestiniog, and the Ffestiniog Toy Railway, or *viâ* Carnarvon. Beddgelert can be approached by the London and North Western line to Dinas Junction, 3 miles south of Carnarvon, thence by the North Wales Narrow Gauge Railway to Snowdon Station,

12½ miles, and thence by coach (several times a day), 4 miles. It can also be approached by rail to Portmadoc or Penrhyndeudraeth. For particulars, *see* excursions from those places.

I. THE ROUTE via CHESTER AND CARNARVON.

The journey from London to Pwllheli occupies about 7½ hours (9.30 to 5.5). Criccieth is reached at 5.8 and Portmadoc at 5.20.

As a large number of the tourists who pass through Chester spend an hour or two within its walls, we will briefly indicate its most interesting features. For hotels in Chester and their tariffs, *see* the Introduction.

Chester

was one of the chief stations of the Romans, by whom it was called Deva, after the river, while the name by which we know the city is the Saxon form of the Latin *castra* (a camp). After the withdrawal of the Romans it was reduced to ruin by the King of Northumbria in 607, and by the Danes in 894. It was rebuilt by Ethelred I., who extended its bounds so as to include the site of the Castle. It was the last place of importance in England to submit to William the Conqueror, who bestowed it upon his nephew, Hugh Lupus, an ancestor of the Grosvenors. On Lupus, William also conferred the dignity of Earl of Chester, a title which has since the time of Henry III. been borne by the heir to the English throne. In the days of Edward I., Chester figured prominently in the wars between the English and the Welsh ; in those of Charles I., it was the first city in the kingdom to declare for the King, and the last to succumb to the Parliamentary forces. In 1659 an unsuccessful attempt was made to garrison it for Charles II., and since then, with the exception of the abortive Fenian raid of 1867, there has been nothing special to record respecting it.

The chief **Railway Station** is the joint property of the London and North-Western and the Great Western Railway Companies. It is three-quarters of a mile from the city itself, which, however, can be easily reached by means of the tramcars (fare threepence), which traverse the streets from end to end every quarter of an hour.

The first glimpse of the quaintness of the city is obtained in Foregate Street, on both sides of which are curious old houses, the upper storeys of some of them built on arches which span the footpaths. In due course we reach

The East Gate

of the city, from very early times its principal means of egress and ingress. On the north-west side are some considerable remains of the original Roman walls. Over the parapet, on the apex of the arch, is a handsome clock, remarkable as being the unaided work of one individual, who spent over two years upon its construction. On the left, in approaching, is a magnificent example of the old timbered style of building.

IN THE ROWS, CHESTER

In Eastgate Street we see one of

The Rows,

the distinguishing architectural feature of Chester. They extend along the greater part of both sides of the four old Roman ways—Eastgate Street, Watergate Street, Northgate Street, and Bridge Street. Covered in by the overhanging upper storeys of the houses, the side walk affords a convenient promenade, protected from sunshine and rain. What we may call the front rooms of the second storeys of the buildings have been removed, and the area occupied by their floors has been flagged for the accommodation of passers-by, while the back rooms have been turned into shops. Leaving Eastgate Street Row by a passage on the right-hand side, we reach

The Cathedral,

formerly the church of a Benedictine Abbey founded by
Hugh Lupus, a nephew of William the Conqueror.

The building was thoroughly restored by Sir Gilbert G.
Scott between 1868 and 1876. It is almost entirely composed
of the red sandstone of the district. The principal portions
were erected during the thirteenth, fourteenth, and fifteenth
centuries, although considerable remains of the original
Norman structure still exist. The western entrance is
formed of a Tudor arch under a square head, and above it
is a fine Perpendicular window. The roof of the **Nave** is com-

CHESTER CATHEDRAL: THE CHOIR

posed of panelled oak, its bosses being ornamented with
coats of arms, mainly of persons closely connected with the
city and its history. Between the baptistery and the north-
east doorway, leading to the cloisters, are very fine mosaics.
Between the nave and the choir is a screen of elaborate wood-
work, and over the stalls in the choir are some of the finest
oak canopies in England. Some of the misereres are very
quaint; all are fully described in Dean Howson's handbook,
price 1s. The richly-carved pulpit in the choir (the gift of
the Freemasons of Cheshire) and the bishop's throne are
also worthy of attention. In the south aisle of the choir is
the shrine of St. Werburgh or Withburga, an Abbess of Ely
in the seventh century, and daughter of Wulpherus, King

of the Mercians. The magnificent painted window of the aisle was the gift of Lord Brassey, as a memorial of his father. The easternmost portion of the cathedral is the **Lady Chapel**. It is entered from the North Choir aisle. On one of its bosses is depicted the murder of Thomas à Becket.

In the **North Transept** is a large modern canopied tomb marking the resting-place of the learned Bishop Pearson, who died in 1686. The **South Transept** is almost as large as the nave, and was formerly the parish church of St. Oswald. On the outside of this portion of the Cathedral, near the south-west angle, are half-length figures of Lord Beaconsfield, Dr. Kenealy, and Mr. Gladstone, the last-named holding his Vatican pamphlets.

The **Cloisters** on the north side of the Cathedral are in the style of the fifteenth century. In the east walk is the entrance to the vestibule of the **Chapter House**, both the vestibule and the chapter room being fine specimens of Early English at its best. In the north walk is the chief entrance to the old **Refectory**, which still contains a fine reader's pulpit approached by a staircase in the wall.

Leaving the Cloisters, and passing beneath the Abbey Gate into Northgate Street, we find ourselves opposite the Market Place, near the site of the very fine **Town Hall** opened by the Prince of Wales in 1869, and partly destroyed by fire in 1897. In Watergate Street are the chief of

The Old Houses.

God's Providence House is so called from the inscription on the front, "God's providence is mine inheritance." It bears the date 1652, but has been rebuilt, the old materials being used as far as possible. Tradition has it that the house was the only dwelling in Chester which was not visited by the plague which devastated the city in the seventeenth century, and that the owner placed the inscription on the front in acknowledgment of his preservation. Mrs. Banks has made use of the tradition in her story, *God's Providence House*.

Farther down the street, and bearing the number twenty nine, is **Bishop Lloyd's House**, famed for its richly-carved front. The prelate was translated from the Manx see to the diocese of Chester in 1605. One of the panels bears his arms and the date 1615.

The **Yacht Inn**, a little farther along the street, is a good specimen of an old English hostelry. Here it was that Dean Swift, annoyed that none of the Cathedral dignitaries responded to his invitation to sup with him, scratched on a window-pane the following sharp couplet:—

> " Rotten without and mouldering within,
> This place and its clergy are nearly akin."

Stanley House, or the Old Palace, formerly a palace of the Stanleys of Alderley, was built in the year 1591, and is the oldest specimen of a house of its kind in Chester. It is reached by way of a small passage on the left after passing Nicholas Street.

Bridge Street, which leads southwards from the Cross to the Bridge Gate, is remarkable for the number of **Roman Remains** found in it. The chief of these is the **Roman Bath**, which is situated below the level of the street, near the site of the old Feathers Hotel. It consists of two rooms in a remarkable state of preservation and easily accessible.

A Walk on the Walls

must be undertaken by those who desire to know Chester. They are the most complete specimen of city walls in England, and give a good idea of what at one time was considered an adequate defence for a populous and wealthy place. They vary in height from twelve to forty feet, and afford an uninterrupted promenade some two

GOD'S PROVIDENCE HOUSE

miles in circumference. The walls may be ascended at either of the four gates, and at other spots. The point of ascent nearest the station is at the East Gate. Making use of that, and turning to the right, the Cathedral is quickly passed, and just beyond it is the **Kale-Yards Gate**, a small passage formed to enable the monks of the convent of St.

Werburgh to get to their kitchen garden, or kale-yard without going round by the East Gate.

A little farther is

The Phœnix, or Newton's Tower

(*admission*, 1*d*.), perhaps the most interesting building in connection with the walls. It takes its name of Phœnix from the crest of a city guild which it bears. As the inscription above its doorway states, King Charles witnessed from this tower the defeat of his army at the battle of Rowton Moor. Leaving the Phœnix Tower

The North Gate

is soon crossed. In its vicinity may be seen some remains of the original Roman walls. They terminate in a cornice six feet below the parapet. Close outside the gate are the Blue Coat Hospital and the Hospital of St. John the Baptist, both old foundations.

Passing on, we come to an ancient watch-tower, known as **Morgan's Mount**, and then to the remains of one formerly called the Goblin Tower, but now **Pemberton's Parlour.** Passing through the latter we see, inside the walls, the **Barrowfield**, once the drill ground of Roman soldiers, and, at a later date, a burial-place for victims of the plague.

KING CHARLES'S TOWER

At the corner, before turning along the south wall, is an edifice, consisting principally of two towers, erected in 1322, the higher one being called **Bonewaldesthorne's** and the lower the **Water Tower**. The former is now used as a museum. In bygone days the river Dee washed against this building, and vessels were moored to rings inserted in the wall.

The West, or Water Gate,

which is reached in due course, is another structure that once had the river flowing close to it, and, like the other gateways, is comparatively new, the date of its erection being 1789. Instead of the river the eye of the spectator now rests on

The Roodee,

a famous but dangerously curved race-course, the drill-ground of the Yeomanry and other troops, and the site of various fêtes. Time was when at every tide this area was flooded, with the exception of one small portion called the Rood Eye, "island of the cross," whence the present name was derived.

Continuing along the walls, we arrive at the building called

The Castle,

and consisting of the Shire Hall, the Assize Court, the Gaol, and the Barracks. Behind the guard-room is a square block known as **Cæsar's Tower**, and interesting as a remnant of the ancient castle. In the vicinity of the castle entrance is the **Grosvenor Museum**, especially noteworthy for its collection of Roman remains, and for its specimens of the birds and insects of Cheshire and North Wales.

Resuming our walk we reach

The South, or Bridge Gate,

which was rebuilt in 1782, and is the gate leading to the **Old Bridge**, a structure dating from the 13th century, and having near it the Dee Mills.

The remaining portion of the walls is uninteresting, and therefore, instead of completing the circuit, the visitor who is not pressed for time will be well advised in proceeding from the Bridge Gate to the river bank, where, by going up the stream, he will pass the **Floating Baths** and the **Landing Stage** (where a boat can be hired for an excursion to Eaton Hall, 5 miles distant) and, ere long, will reach the **Suspension Bridge**. There, turning to the left, he will have on his right **Grosvenor Park**, a public recreation ground, and on the other side will see

The Church of St. John the Baptist,

next to the Cathedral the most interesting ecclesiastical edifice in the city. It was begun about 1075, and was intended for the cathedral of the diocese that included Lichfield and Chester, but Coventry was chosen to be the seat of the bishop. A steeple which occupied a central position fell about the middle of the fifteenth century and crushed the east end, which was never rebuilt. In 1881 a tower at the west end fell and did much injury, including the destruction of the north porch, which was rebuilt in 1883. The north-east clock tower and belfry were erected in 1887, and the west window was presented in 1890 by the late Duke of West-minster. It illustrates the history of the city from the massacre of the monks of Bangor-is-y-coed, in 613, to the Restoration of Episcopacy in 1660.

In the immediate neighbourhood of the church, but in private grounds, are the ruins of St. John's Priory.

By following Little St. John Street and then St. John Street to the right the visitor will quickly arrive at Foregate Street and the East Gate.

FROM CHESTER TO CARNARVON.

As far as Rhyl, a popular watering-place some 30 miles from Chester, the railway traveller has the choice of two routes. One runs along the coast, the other passes through Mold, Denbigh, and St. Asaph. The former is

(a) THE DIRECT ROUTE,

and forms part of the main route to Holyhead.

Leaving Chester Station the line first skirts the Dee, affording a splendid view of the Roodee, and then, crossing the river, enters Wales.

A little short of the third station—Connah's Quay—we pass under the railway bridge carrying a line from Chester to Hawarden. The fourth station is at Flint, fourteen miles from Chester. On the marsh are the remains of an ancient castle connected with important events in English history. Nearly three miles farther is Holywell, taking its name from its well of Saint Winifred. Passing Mostyn and Prestatyn, Great Orme's Head comes into view, with Penmaenmawr to the east of it, and we soon arrive at Rhyl.

(b) Vîâ MOLD, DENBIGH, AND ST. ASAPH.

Leaving the Chester and Holyhead Railway at a distance of three miles from Chester, this branch line runs past Broughton Hall, one of the stations for Hawarden, to Hope Exchange, 9½ miles, and at twelve miles from Chester reaches Mold, a town of some 4,500 inhabitants, who are principally engaged in mining and agriculture. About five miles to the west is Moel Fammau just over 1,800 feet in height. It is a prominent object in the view along either route.

The third station beyond Mold is at Caerwys, twenty-two miles from Chester. Though now an insignificant place, it was originally the site of a Roman station. A short distance farther is Bodfari, where we enter the Vale of Clwyd;

and then comes Denbigh, twenty-nine miles from our starting point. Then a run of five miles brings us to St. Asaph, and at the end of another six miles we are at **Rhyl**.

Westward from Rhyl.

Leaving Rhyl and proceeding in a westerly direction for a little over four miles, we reach **Abergele** and **Pensarn**, the latter being near the station, and the former about a mile away. Immediately beyond the station, a modern mansion called Gwrych Castle, situated on a hill-side on the left, attracts attention. It is the seat of Lord Dundonald, who gained fame in connection with the relief of Ladysmith. Some six miles farther we run through a tunnel in the headland of Penmaen Rhos, and then reach in quick succession the quiet village of **Old Colwyn** and the popular resort of **Colwyn Bay**, eleven miles from Rhyl. Four-and-a-half miles farther we arrive at **Llandudno Junction** (*refreshment rooms*), from which a branch line runs northwards to **Llandudno**, three miles distant, and another goes southward to Bettws-y-Coed and Blaenau Ffestiniog.

Almost immediately after leaving Llandudno Junction, on its way westward, the line crosses the mouth of the river Conway by a bridge of similar construction to the celebrated Britannia Bridge over the Menai Straits. The masonry is designed to harmonise with the adjoining ruins of Conway Castle.

On leaving **Conway** we have on the right Conway Morfa, much used in summer as a camping ground for volunteer battalions, and on the left the mountains of Snowdonia. The extremity of the range at this point is called Penmaen-bach, and the line passes through it by a tunnel a few yards westward of which is the spot, where, early in 1899, the railway track was completely carried away by a great sea, and a train precipitated into the water.

Less than five miles from Conway we reach **Penmaenmawr**, a pleasant, quiet seaside resort, named from the adjacent precipitous headland through which the railway pierces by means of a tunnel. At the end of three miles we reach the village of **Llanfairfechan**, and two miles farther west arrive at **Aber**, a village famed for its waterfall.

Continuing our journey for some three miles, we then obtain glimpses of Penrhyn Castle on the right.

After crossing two viaducts which span the Ogwen River and Valley, we pass through a tunnel, which pierces the Bangor Mountain, and soon find ourselves at **Bangor**, five miles from Aber, and sixty from Chester. (*Refreshment rooms on both platforms.*)

Bangor is the point in the Cambrian Railways Company's excursion to Beaumaris from Pwllheli, Criccieth, and Portmadoc at which tourists leave the rail. From Bangor they go by coach over the Menai Suspension Bridge to Beaumaris, 6½ miles. Its chief object of interest is the Castle. The coach returns from Beaumaris at 5.0 p.m. The passengers may break their journey at Bangor or at Beaumaris, and proceed within three days by coach or rail. Both Bangor and Beaumaris are fully described in our *Guide to the Northern Section of North Wales.*

From Bangor to Carnarvon, between eight and nine miles, the line skirts the Menai Straits. The first station is **Menai Bridge.** It is near the famous Suspension Bridge. Proceeding, we obtain good views of the Strait and its bridges, of the Anglesey Monument, and near Treborth, the second station, we may get a glimpse of the peak of Snowdon. After passing the next station, **Port Dinorwic,** we may see, on the Anglesey shore, the fine mansion of Plas-Newydd, the seat of the Marquis of Anglesey, and at 68½ miles from Chester we reach **Carnarvon.**

From Carnarvon

the train runs southwards at an increasing distance from the west coast. By looking backwards on the right immediately on resuming the journey, we get a good view of Carnarvon Castle. At the end of 3½ miles we come to **Dinas Station,** the junction with the North Wales narrow-gauge railway to Snowdon Station. Another run of equal length brings us to **Pen-y-Groes,** interesting only to the tourist as the junction for **Nantlle** (*nant-thly*), 1½ miles distant, famed for the magnificent view it affords of Snowdon. Beyond this junction the scenery is uninteresting. At **Pantglas,** 10½ miles from Carnarvon, the line reaches its highest point, 180 feet, and about a couple of miles farther Moel Hebog comes in sight, with Snowdon visible over its shoulder. At a distance of 19 miles from Carnarvon we arrive at **Afon Wen** (*refreshment rooms*), the junction of the London and North-Western and Cambrian lines. From that, Pwllheli lies 1½ miles to the west, Criccieth 3½ miles to the east, and Portmadoc 5 miles farther.

II. THE ROUTE via BALA

has been described as far as **Bala Junction**. From the junction we proceed to the town, three-quarters of a mile distant, and described on p. 189. On leaving the town, we at once enter the Tryweryn Valley, and get a view of the Arenig Mountains. They can conveniently be ascended from **Arenig** Station, which we pass 8 miles from Bala, and beyond which we pass through uninteresting scenery to the highest point of the line, 1,196 feet, near **Llyn Tryweryn**. Thence, as we proceed, the Rhinogs come into view in front, and Cader Idris in the south. A little beyond **Trawsfynydd** we may see, on the right, the two-headed green mound called Tomen-y-mur, referred to on p. 166, and in front may be seen Moelwyn and other peaks rising from the other side of the Vale of Ffestiniog. This beautiful vale comes into sight on the left, as soon as we have passed the next station, and thence the view is charming as we pass through **Ffestiniog Village** and along the hillside for 3½ miles farther to **Blaenau Ffestiniog** (25½ miles from Bala Junction), where we must "change" for the "Toy" railway.

III. THE ROUTE via BETTWS-Y-COED.

By this route we leave the main line at Llandudno Junction, and pass thence through pretty scenery along the eastern bank of the Conway River. We pass stations at Glan Conway, Tal-y-Cafn, and Llanrwst, and then reach **Bettws-y-Coed**, 15 miles from the junction. It is situated in the midst of such charming scenery that it fully deserves its title of the "Paradise of Wales."

At the station are brakes and private carriages to convey visitors to the **Miners' Bridge** (1 mile), the **Swallow Waterfalls** (2½ miles), and to the **Fairy Glen** (1½ miles). Brake fare, 1). These and other delightful excursions from it, as well as the village itself, are fully described in our *Guide to the Northern Section of North Wales*.

Bettws-y-Coed is a point in one of the Cambrian Railways Company's Excursions from Pwllheli, Criccieth, and Portmadoc. Passengers are conveyed to it by rail *via* Afon Wen, Carnarvon, and Llandudno Junction. The distance by this route, from Pwllheli to Bettws-y-Coed, is 62 miles. From Bettws-y-Coed the passengers are conveyed by coach through the far-famed Pass of Llanberis, to the village of Llanberis, a distance of 16 miles, and thence proceed by train to their destination, *via* Carnarvon. The distance from Llanberis to Pwllheli by rail is 22½ miles. Passengers have the option of breaking their journey at Bettws-y-Coed or Llanberis, and proceeding within three days.

After leaving Bettws-y-Coed, the line soon enters the valley of the Lledr. Here we have most delightful scenery, and on the right get a glorious view of Moel Siabod (*shab-bod*), which is best ascended from Dolwyddelen Station, 5¾ miles from Bettws-y-Coed. A short two miles farther brings us to the station called **Roman Bridge**, a most misleading name, for the structure is quite modern. For another 1½ miles we go through the valley, and on emerging from a tunnel, have but a short run to Blaenau Ffestiniog (12½ miles from Bettws-y-Coed), where we change for the "Toy" railway.

NANTLLE VALE, FROM DRWS-Y-COED

STILL POOL, BETTWS-Y-COED

IV. THE ROUTE BY THE CAMBRIAN COAST LINE.

This has been described as far as **Harlech**. Just beyond Harlech we pass the small station of **Talsarnau**, from which, by looking west, we get a good view of **Deudraeth Castle**, a modern mansion, standing on the site of an old-world fortalice, which has supplied the neighbouring village with the affix distinguishing it from other Penrhyns (or headlands) in Wales.

Penrhyn-Deudraeth,

16¼ miles from Barmouth and 15¼ from Pwllheli, is the nearest station on the Cambrian line to Maentwrog and Tan-y-Bwlch. It is also a station on the Ffestiniog "Toy" railway. From it conveyances run in connection with excursions organized by the Cambrian Railways Company.

Just a mile farther is **Minffordd Junction**, the "exchange station" between the Cambrian and Ffestiniog lines. Then, having passed over a long embankment, constructed for the reclamation of the low-lying land on the right, we come to **Portmadoc**, 19¼ miles from Barmouth, and still keeping close to the coast, presently see **Criccieth Castle** on the left, with the modest esplanade at its foot. Beyond that there is nothing of special interest. Stations at Afon Wen and Abererch follow that at Criccieth, and then comes **Pwllheli**.

PWLLHELI.

Banks.—The *National Provincial of England*, the *North and South Wales*, and the *Metropolitan of England and Wales*.

Bathing Machines.—Each person, 3*d.* ; with use of bathing dress, 6*d.*

Boats.—*Row boats*, **6***d.* per hour for each person ; boatman, 6*d.* per hour. *Sailing boats*, 2/6 per hour. Fare to St. Tudwall's Isle, **2/-**.

Distances by Rail.

	MILES.		MILES.		MILES.
Barmouth ...	32	Carnarvon... ...	23	London *via*	
Birmingham *via*		Chester	91	Shrewsbury ...	280
Chester	157	Liverpool	110	Portmadoc... ...	13
Birmingham *via*		London *via*			
Shrewsbury ...	159	Chester	269		

Fishing.—*See* Appendix for Anglers.

Golf.—*See* Appendix for Golfers.

Hotels.—*See* Introduction.

London Papers arrive about 2.0 ; Provincial, about 10.0.

Omnibuses.—Between the station and the town.

Places of Worship, with the hours of English service on Sundays:—
St. Peter's Church, 11.0 and 7.30.
English Presbyterian, Ala Road, 10.30 and 6.0.
Penlan Congregational, 11.0.
South Beach New Calvinistic Methodist, 10.30 and 6.0.
Roman Catholic, North Street, 8.0 and 11.0.

Population.—About 4,000.

Post Office. The chief office is in High Street (in the old town). Branch office, South Beach.

Recreation.—Angling and sea fishing; golf; and in the Recreation Ground, Cardiff Road, tennis, and cricket clubs.

Tours. Intending visitors may obtain much assistance in planning and making arrangements for tours in North Wales, by stating their wants and sending a stamped addressed envelope to the Town Clerk, hon. sec. of the Welsh Touring Association, Pwllheli.

The formidable name, Pwllheli (*poolth-helly*) means "the salt-water pit." The place which bears it is the northern terminus of the Cambrian Railways. It is a busy little seaport, the market town of a large agricultural district, and what is more to the purpose of our readers, a seaside resort looking down on Cardigan Bay, and enjoying a large measure of popularity on account of the salubrity of its climate, its magnificent beach, and the diversified character of the surrounding scenery. The town was made a free borough by the Black Prince. It is still governed by its own mayor and corporation, and now consists of an "old town" (the main street of which has been widened and vastly improved to meet the increased demands upon it) and a "new town" on the south beach, the two being about ten minutes' walk apart.

Pwllheli is the business centre of the great peninsula which is generally called

The Lleyn Promontory,

much of which is little trodden by the tourist, and having many spots where no word of English is spoken or understood.

For the most part, the mountains and hills, which form such a striking feature when seen from a distant view-point, decline in elevation from east to west, and when viewed singly are not, in themselves, particularly attractive. From the summit of most there is a grand panorama of land and sea, and for the sake of these prospects they are worth ascending.

Much of the district is divided into small holdings, and cattle-rearing and pig-breeding are largely followed.

But, as Bradley says in his *Highways and Byways of North Wales*, "What is now an *Ultima Thule* was, a thousand years ago, a land trodden by the feet of strangers from every shore of the Irish Sea—missionaries, hostile invaders, and pious pilgrims. Every church recalls some Celtic saint, and marks a stage upon the pilgrim track. . . . The pilgrims were on their way to Bardsey" which has been aptly described as the Iona of Wales.

Only 120 years ago,

Pwllheli Harbour

was used by more vessels than went to that of the more important town of Carnarvon. But by the action of the sea the harbour has become so choked with sand as, at low tide, to be almost dry. The deposit, however, is about to be removed, so that the basin may be used, not only for trading purposes, but as a harbour of refuge.

The local authorities are extremely enterprising, and are desirous of effecting many

Improvements.

Among other things, it is intended to construct a caisson, with sluice gates, to keep the water in the harbour during the daytime, in order to improve the already excellent opportunities for pleasure-boating. When this is done, the harbour will form a splendid lake of salt water about a hundred acres in extent. Some day Pwllheli is to be illumined at night by the electric light, electric cars are to run through the streets and for some distance into the surrounding country, and other attractions are to be added, in order to make the town a model summer and winter resort. And the directors of the Cambrian Railways are to help on the good work by removing the railway station, now on the outskirts, into the centre of the town.

New Pwllheli

consists of two distinct districts, known respectively as **South Beach** and the **West End**. It is about a mile from the old town, with which each part, however, is connected by a tram-line. (Fare to South Beach or to West End, 1*d*.) Each has a fine promenade and sea-wall, elegant marine residences and hotels, first-class boarding houses and lodging houses. (There are also good hotels in the old town.)

On a fine day the view from the shore extends, with the aid of a glass, as far as Aberystwyth, right opposite; Harlech Castle and Cader Idris appear on the left side, and from the rear Snowdon and the Rivals can be seen.

The Beach,

one of the very finest in the kingdom, extends westward from the **Gimlet Rock**, a natural curiosity, at the mouth of the harbour, to a wooded headland near Llanbedrog, a distance of 5 miles. It is composed of sand and small shingle, has the advantage of a southerly aspect, stretches out evenly, and is of such gradual and uniform slope that bathing may be enjoyed at all states of the tide. The water only recedes a few yards. The shore yields rare and valuable shells to the conchologist.

In the old town,

The Parish Church

is the most attractive object. It was consecrated in 1887 and dedicated to St. Peter. It is a beautiful example of the Early Decorated style, and exhibits some of the leading features of the ancient Welsh churches. As is usual in them, the chancel is a continuation of the nave, without any break in the walls or in the roof, the east end being furnished with a panelled ceiling, or mwd, as it is called in Welsh.

Mention has been made of the salubrity of

The Climate

of Pwllheli. The town has a southern aspect, and is enclosed by a semicircle of mountains, which effectually screen it from the cold north and east winds. Pwllheli has been called the Riviera of Wales, and, considered solely with respect to its climatic conditions, it well deserves the name. It is hardly necessary to say that the place has not the gaiety of the French Riviera, but it has all that is essential to health. The air is dry and pure, and in the summer the heat is tempered by pleasant breezes.

According to the figures prepared by Mr. Alexander Buchan, F.R.S.E., based on calculations extending over twenty years, the winter and early spring temperature of Pwllheli is as mild as that of Torquay, Bournemouth, or the Isle of Wight, and the air is not so relaxing.

Everywhere there is ocular evidence of the mildness of the winters at Pwllheli, for the myrtle, fuchsia, and hydrangea flourish profusely in the open air.

Dr. A. Dowling Prendergast, M.D., M.Ch., M.A.O., Royal University of Ireland, and Doctor of Sanitary Science,

PWLLHELI

PWLLHELI HARBOUR

Victoria University, writes as follows: " Pwllheli, without doubt, possesses all the requisite essentials for a health resort."

The Water Supply

is excellent, and is sufficient for a population more than twice as large as that which it at present serves. It is obtained from mountains 4 miles inland.

Pwllheli is not without its

Attractions for Sportsmen.

There is good trout fishing in the immediate neighbourhood, and there is good shooting during the autumn. There are thousands of acres of marsh and rough uplands, and leave to shoot over them can be obtained without much difficulty. The marshes are intersected by small swamps, pools, and lagoons, which are the haunts of large numbers of long-winged fowl and surface-feeders. As the climate is milder than any other centre so far north, birds are more attracted to it, while the hardships of winter shooting are lessened.

The Drives and Walks

in the vicinity are very fine. Many of them present considerable attractions to the antiquarian, as several Roman fortresses and other old-world remains may be examined. The scenery from the summits of the neighbouring mountains is very beautiful, and as the heights are easily accessible, even for children and delicate persons, they present a good ground for picnic parties and the like.

SHORT WALKS FROM PWLLHELI.

1. THE PANORAMA WALK.

This is a very popular walk close to the town. It is reached by way of Ala Road, and passes through the beautiful nurseries of Messrs. Dickson. About midway is a rock from which may be obtained a charming view over sea and land.

2. TO PEN-Y-GARN.

Pen-y-Garn is a peak rising immediately above the town, from which it is reached by way of Salem Terrace, up the hill to which that leads, and then through the second gateway on the left. The summit commands an extensive view of the Snowdonian range, the Rivals, and the coast of Merionethshire.

Pedestrians who feel equal to a longer walk should pass on from Pen-y-Garn to the left of Denio church and cemetery, towards Caenaugwynion river, where they will find a rustic bridge and pretty scenery. On returning, visitors must retrace their steps for a short distance, and then the route may be varied by taking the first turning on the right after leaving Caenaugwynion road. This will lead them past a couple of mills to the high road to Llannor. By proceeding along that to the left they are brought to

THE PARADE AND WEST END HOTEL, PWLLHELI

the village of Efailnewydd, 2 miles from Pwllheli, which is reached by following the Nevin high road.

3. TO ABERERCH BEACH.

This is a particularly bracing tract to the east of Pwllheli. To reach it, follow the Abererch road, and then the cross-road past the Cambrian Railways station.

EXCURSIONS FROM PWLLHELI.

Unless they can book their seats on the private brakes and chars-a-banc of private proprietors, visitors are strongly advised to make their excursions from Pwllheli under the auspices of the Cambrian Railways Co., otherwise they will have to scramble for a seat, and may fail to obtain one.

1. TO LLANBEDROG, 1 miles.

By tramway from the town to the beach at the West End, and thence along the coast. Fare to Llanbedrog only, 4d. Combined tickets, including return and admission to Glyn-y-weddw Hall Art Gallery and Gardens, 1/-. Children under six, half-price. There is a booking office on the beach at West End. Tickets are also obtainable on the cars.

Glyn-y-Weddw Hall

was the picturesque country residence of Sir Love Jones Parry, Bart. On one of the stained-glass windows is the

GLYN-Y-WEDDW HALL

following inscription. "This house was built by Lady Jones Parry, widow of Sir Love Parry Jones Parry, 1857." It is now owned by Messrs. Andrews, the proprietors of much of New Pwllheli. The estate covers about 50 acres, and is situated at the end of Llanbedrog Bay. It is so sheltered that camellias and other delicate trees and shrubs remain in the open air all the year round. Visitors are at liberty to walk or sit in the lovely gardens, and to wander along the rustic paths, in the woods on the sides of the mountains. The collection of pictures is large and varied, and includes some of the productions of the most eminent artists.

Concerts and other entertainments are given in a hall

which has been specially built for the purpose, and there is a large refreshment room.

Llanbedrog Hill, 433 feet, overlooks the village. To reach the summit, take the first turn to the left past the church.

2. THROUGH BODVEAN WOODS TO NEVIN AND PORTDINLLAEN.

1. By brake leaving Pwllheli at 2.30 p.m. one day a week. Return fare, 2/.
2. By coach running in connection with the Cambrian Railways Company. It leaves the station *daily* at 10.50, calls at the Crown Hotel, and then goes on to Nevin, returning in time for the 4 p.m. train. Holders of tickets from other stations on the Cambrian line may return to the starting-point by any through train on the date of the issue of the ticket, or on the following day.
3. By char-a-banc from the Eifl Hotel, High Street, on Monday, Wednesday, and Thursday, at 2.15, for Bodvean Woods only. Return fare, 1/3.

Not long after leaving Pwllheli, we pass **Bodvel Hall**, interesting to many visitors as having for a time been the abode of Mrs. Piozzi, better known, perhaps, as Mrs. Thrale, who, with her first husband, enjoyed the friendship of Dr. Johnson, who once spent a few days here as her guest.

The Bodvean Woods,

About 4 miles from Pwllheli, are of great extent. They surround the seat of the Hon. F. G. Wynn. The public road runs through the heart of them. On emerging from the woods, we find ourselves on the Portmadoc road. By turning to the left we again come to the Pwllheli and Nevin road, which was quitted on entering the woods. Turning to the left, we soon pass Bodvean Church, and some 2 miles beyond the woods reach

Nevin,

an extensive fishing town situated on the southern shore of the Bay of Carnarvon. The beach is one of the finest in Wales. It is composed of firm, clean sand, and affords safe and pleasant bathing. Visitors may also enjoy safe boating in the little bay fronting the town. The climate is mild, but bracing. The scenery is magnificent. In the immediate neighbourhood there are pleasant cliff walks, and the surrounding district affords interesting excursions and mountain climbing.

Nevin is 4 miles from the Rival Mountains and Vortigern's Valley. It is 7 miles from Pwllheli Station, on the Cambrian Railway, and 10 miles from Chwilog Station, on the London and North-Western line. At both stations conveyances meet the principal trains.

Nevin is historically interesting as the spot where, in 1284, Edward I. held a grand triumphal festival, at which a round table and tournaments were the principal amusements. The site of the lists can still be traced. The *Church* (*St. Mary's*) has a singularly narrow tower, surmounted by a disproportionate ship, which does duty for a weathercock. Nevin is an ancient borough, of which Lord Newborough is hereditary mayor. Some day or other the Cambrian Railways Company hope to carry their line to Port Dinlleyn, near Nevin, and to open out a new route thence to Dublin.

3. TO ABERDARON.

1. By brake from Pwllheli, at 9.0 a.m., on one day of the week, returning from Aberdaron at 3.0 p.m. Return fare, 3/.
2. By char-a-banc from Elil Hotel, High Street, on Saturdays, at 9.30. Return fare, 3/.

The outward journey is through the Valley of Nanhoron and through Sarn. The return is made over the Rhiw Mountain. Distance, about 35 miles.

There is very little in the scenery along the route to command admiration. The most attractive spot is

The Nanhoron Valley,

which lies to the south-west of Pwllheli, at a distance of about 8 miles. It is diversified by woods and meadows, and is backed by Carn Madryn.

Thence the route continues in a westerly direction for another 3½ miles to a pretty hamlet called **Sarn**.

On Mynydd Cefn Amwlch, 2 miles to the north by west of Sarn, is a cromlech remarkable for its peaked cap-stone.

At Sarn the road turns to the south-west, and at the end of some 4 miles passes **Castell Odo**, an ancient camp. 1½ miles beyond which is

Aberdaron,

at the extremity of the peninsula, some 16½ miles from Pwllheli by the shortest route (*via* Rhiw). It is a small and not very attractive village, situated on the seashore, but protected by gradually rising cliffs. It was the birthplace of an eccentric individual named Richard Robert Jones, who became better known as Dick of Aberdaron. He acquired thirteen or fourteen languages, but could make no profitable use of them. He was always in great poverty, and used to parade the streets of Liverpool extremely dirty and ragged, with some mutilated stores of literature under his arm. He was born in 1788, and died at St. Asaph in 1845.

2½ miles beyond Aberdaron is the cape known as **Braich-y-Pwll** (*brak-e-pool*),

The " Land's End of Wales,"

where is magnificent cliff scenery. On the shore, to the east of the extreme point, and approachable only at low water, is **Ffynnon Fair**, "Our Lady's Well," which always yields fresh water, although it is often covered by the sea. The credulous may test the reputed virtues of the water to obtain the fulfilment of a wish, by running, with mouth filled with the liquid, three times round the quadrangle of an old abbey hard by.

The country around is particularly delightful when the gorse or the heather is in bloom. 2 miles off the Cape is

Bardsey Isle,

a conspicuous object in the seascape from most parts of the coast of Cardigan Bay. It is some 19½ miles from Pwllheli. On it are the scanty remains of an Abbey founded in the 5th century. On account of its supposed peculiar sanctity, the island was a favourite burial place. The last person of importance interred in its soil was a Lord Newborough, who had erected a monument to those previously buried there. A Celtic cross of white Anglesey marble, 28 feet high, has been erected to the memory of the noble lord, and another monument has also been set up in honour of "the saints."

By reason of a strong current the island can be reached or left only when wind and tide are both favourable, and as several days sometimes pass without these conditions being fulfilled, visitors who go to Aberdaron purposely to visit the island should be prepared for detention. A mile from the landing-place is a small portion of the tower of the Abbey of St. Mary, dating from the 13th century.

The inhabitants of the island occupy some half a dozen farmsteads, and add fishing to their cultivation of the land. Tuesday is the day on which some of them generally visit the mainland. They are a hardy race, "paying," we are told, "their rent to Lord Newborough, the owner of the land, but beyond that owning no government but their own. They cultivate a spirit of mutual independence, and elect from among themselves a king, who also discharges the duties of minister."

Returning from Aberdaron

we keep along the coast, and pass through grand and rugged scenery to **Rhiw**, which gives its name to a neighbouring height (965 feet) which presents much to interest geologists and botanists, and commands a magnificent view of the surrounding country. Near Rhiw the road attains an elevation of 615 feet. At the summit of the pass is a roadside inn. At Rhiw the road leaves the sea and strikes across to Llanbedrog, near which we pass through Pig Street. From Llanbedrog the road is again at no great distance from the sea.

4. TO LLITHFAEN FOR VORTIGERN'S VALLEY AND THE RIVALS.

By brake from Pwllheli once a week, at 11.30. Return fare, 3/ .

A pleasant drive through country lanes brings us in little more than an hour to the small village of **Llithfaen**, a convenient starting-place for the ascent of the Eifl Mountains, called by the English

The Rivals,

whose triple head presents such a surprisingly bold appearance from land and sea. From Llithfaen, the highest of the three peaks (1,849 feet) can be reached in about three-quarters of an hour. On one side the view extends from Great Ormes Head to Pembrokeshire, and on the other to the Wicklow Hills in Ireland.

On the peak which stands between the highest summit and the road from Llithfaen to Carnarvon is **Tre'r Ceiri**, "the Giants' Town," the most important of the pre-historic towns in North Wales. Parts of the enclosing wall are 15 feet high, and the diameter of some of the circular dwellings is 15 or 16 feet. The site is best reached from the Carnarvon road, about half a mile from Llithfaen. A description of the remains will be found in the *Archæologia Cambrensis for* 1871 (*4th series, vol. II.*).

Vortigern's Valley

lies between the Rivals and the sea. It owes its name to its legendary connection with the death of that British chieftain. One story says it was the site of Vortigern's Castle, which was destroyed by lightning. Another tells how Vortigern fled to this spot for refuge from his subjects, and on being discovered leapt into the sea. The rock from which he is said to have taken the fatal leap rises some 450 feet sheer from the sea, and is called Careg-y-Llam (Rock of the Leap). Some colour was given to the tradition that the valley was his burial place by the discovery, more than 100 years ago, of a stone coffin containing the skeleton of a man of more than ordinary size, but a rock on the Teifi is named by the earliest authority as the spot from which Vortigern made his exit.

Visitors may have a difficulty in discovering the valley if they ask for it by its English name. **Nant Gwrtheyrn** is the native name of the valley, and **Bedd Gwrtheyrn** (the Grave of Vortigern), that of the tumulus from which the coffin was removed.

The Return Journey is made by another route. Two miles from Llithfaen we come to **Llanaelhaiarn**, just short of which is **St. Aelhairn's Well**, which, a tablet states, was " roofed " in 1900.

On the coast, 4 miles beyond Llanaelhaiarn, is **Clynnog**, with a fine church restored in 1858. Pennant described it as " the most magnificent structure of the kind in North Wales."

The scenery along the homeward route is pleasant, but not remarkable.

5. TO GARN FADRYN OR MADRYN MOUNTAIN.

By brake from Pwllheli once a week, at 1.30 p.m. Return fare, including admission at Glyn Weddw Hall, 2/6.

Garn Fadryn,

or Madryn Mountain, is 1,217 feet in height, and is the second loftiest point in the Lleyn peninsula, being exceeded only by the Rivals. Tradition says that King Arthur held his famous Round Table Conference on its summit. Nestling under the north side of the hill is **Madryn Castle**, once the seat of Sir Love Jones Parry, Bart., the former owner, it will be remembered, of Llanbedrog. Visitors who obtain a permit are admitted to the gardens in the absence of the family. Garn Fadryn is about 8 miles from Pwllheli.

Pedestrians can save a couple of miles by taking the tram to Llanbedrog.

The Return Journey is made through **Nanhoron Valley**, over Mynytho, and by Glyn Weddw Hall.

6. TO ABERSOCH, 7 miles.

A coach running under the auspices of the Cambrian Railways Co. leaves Pwllheli Station at 10.50 daily (Sundays excepted), calls at the Crown Hotel, and returns in time for the 4.0 p.m. train.

The village can also be reached by taking the tramcar to Llanbedrog, and then walking 3 miles.

The ride to Abersoch takes about an hour. The whole of the route lies through the loveliest scenery. The views include Snowdon, Cader Idris, Moel Hebog, Moel Wynn, Cynicht, and the Rivals.

Abersoch

is a small, quiet watering-place, one of the chief charms of which is its extreme simplicity. It stands on the shore of a pretty little bay, whose extensive sands afford good bathing, but the tide recedes to **a great** distance. From full to half-tide, swimmers will find deep water under Benar Hill. Visitors must beware of being surrounded by the tide at this point. Those who care to spend a day fishing for mackerel may make arrangements for hiring or accompanying one of the numerous roomy boats belonging to the little port; but, on account of the currents, it is not advisable, even for skilled yachtsmen, to venture alone beyond the bay. In the stream from which the village takes its name there is good trout-fishing, except in very dry seasons.

One mile distant is the quaint village of **Llanengan,** which contains one of the most ancient churches in the peninsula. It has a richly-carved screen, considered by some to be the finest in Wales. It has also a chest of solid oak, which, in olden days, served as a safe.

About a mile west of Abersoch is **Pen-y-gaer,** from which is obtained a good view of **Hell's Mouth,** a broad, sandy bay, which owes its name to the danger it is to shipping—a danger partly due to its currents. In stormy weather, the sea at this spot is very fine.

Less than a mile from the shore are **St. Tudwall's Island and lighthouse.** Boats to visit them can be obtained on easy terms. Three miles from Abersoch is Nanhoron Valley (*see* No. 3).

7. THROUGH THE NANHORON VALLEY,

returning over Mynytho, and visiting Glyn-y-Weddw Hall.

A brake leaves Pwllheli once a week at 2.30 p.m. Return fare, including admission to the grounds and art galleries, 2/6.

8. TO BEDDGELERT, 42 miles.

Daily by rail to Portmadoc at 9.50, and thence by conveyance, running under the auspices of the Cambrian Railways Co. It returns from Beddgelert at 2.30. Return fare, 4/3. By this route visitors are sure of a seat in the road conveyance, and can take advantage of a fine day.

By brake from Pwllheli at least once a week, leaving at 9 a.m., and returning from Beddgelert at 4.30 p.m. Return fare, 3/6.

The coach route at first runs eastward, and soon passes through Abererch. A few miles farther it reaches **Llanystum-dwy** and another 2 miles brings us to **Criccieth.**

Thus far the road has been close to the railway and the sea, but beyond Criccieth it lies farther from the coast, and at the end of 42 miles reaches

Tremadoc,

a village which takes its name from its founder, W. A. Maddocks, at one time M.P. for Boston, who succeeded, between 1798 and 1811, in reclaiming from the sea a wide sandy estuary, and a tract of boggy country, called Penmorfa Marsh. To expedite the work, he constructed an embankment across the front of the estuary, and carried along it the present high-road, connecting the counties of Carnarvon and Merioneth. Having succeeded in his undertaking, he built the village at the foot of a high mountain on the western side of the reclaimed land.

The Road from Tremadoc

to Beddgelert commands a series of fine views. Proceeding in a north-easterly direction, we have on our right the **Traeth Mawr,** with the Glaslyn flowing through it. A run of 2½ miles brings us to **Glaslyn Inn,** where a footpath from Portmadoc joins the road. From the inn our route takes a northerly direction for 3 miles close to the stream, and then enters the beautiful

Pass of Aberglaslyn,

which is bounded on each side by mountains of great height. The bridge, **Pont Aberglaslyn,** which here spans the stream, is a single-arched, ivy-clad structure ascribed to Satanic agency. It leads at the end of a mile and a half to **Beddgelert.**

EXCURSIONS BY RAIL AND ROAD FROM PWLLHELI

under the auspices of the Cambrian Railways Company.

Further particulars are given in connection with the place at which passengers leave the main line, as indicated in the last of the following columns. The excursions are also available for visitors at Criccieth and Portmadoc, and, for the most part, for those near the minor stations on this section of the line. The train times are only given for the general information of the reader. Reference should be made to the current Programme of Excursions issued by the Cambrian Railways Co.

NEVIN AND THE RIVALS

THE PASS OF ABERGLASLYN

Short Title.	Train leaves Pwllheli.	Fare : Coach and 3rd class rail.	Described in this Guide as an excursion from
Dinas Mawddwy to Corris* .	7.0	8/6	Cemmes Rd.
,, ,, Dolgelley	7.0	7/3	,,
Corris to Dolgelley * . .	7.0	7/3	Machynlleth
,, Dinas Mawddwy* .	7.0	8/6	,,
Dolgelley to Dinas Mawddwy	11.15	7/3	Dolgelley
,, Corris* .	11.15	7/3	,,
Mochras or Shell Island .	9.50	4 -	Pensarn
Cynicht (Sugar-loaf Mountain) . . .	9.50	3 6	Penrhyn Deudraeth
Llyfnant Valley . . .	6.20, 11.15	5 6	Glandovey
Devil's Bridge . . .	6.20	9/-	Aberystwyth
Tan-y-Bwlch and Maentwrog	9.50	4 -	Penrhyn Deudraeth
Foot of Snowdon . . .	9.50	5 6	,,
Tal-y-Llyn Lake, *viâ* Towyn .	6.20	6 -	Towyn
,, ,, *viâ* Corris .	6.20, 7.0, 9.50	6/3	Machynlleth
,, ,, *viâ* Corris and Towyn .	9.50	7 3	Towyn
Cader Idris	6.20	6 -	,,
The Happy Valley . . .	9.50	6/-	,,
Torrent Walk	6.20	4 6	Dolgelley
Precipice and Torrent Walks .	6.20	5 9	,,
Torrent Walk and Tynygroes	6.20	7 3	,,
Cwm Bychan Lake . .	9.50	4 3	Pensarn
Beddgelert . . .	9.50	4 3	Portmadoc and Penrhyn Deudraeth
Loop Tour around Snowdon .	7.0	11 6	Carnarvon
Beaumaris	7.0	7/-	Bangor
Llanberis and Bettws-y-Coed	7.0	11 6	Bettws-y-Coed
Snowdon, *viâ* North Wales Narrow Gauge * . .	9.50	4 6	Portmadoc and Penrhyn Deudraeth

* Part of the journey is accomplished on a miniature railway.

Cycling and Walking Tours.

Tickets at reduced fares for a fortnight from the date of issue are issued from Pwllheli for use between that station and others which are specified in the programme of excursions.

Day Excursion Tickets

are issued, for ordinary trains, every weekday during the season at the rate of about a halfpenny per mile.

Circular Tour by Rail.

Every weekday cheap tickets (3rd class, 6/3) are issued to enable visitors to make a circular tour through Portmadoc, Harlech, Barmouth, Bala, Ffestiniog, and Blaenau Ffestiniog. They are available on the day of issue and the following day, and the journey may be broken at *any* station.

CRICCIETH.

Angling.—*See* Appendix for Anglers.

Banks.—*National Provincial of England, Metropolitan of England and Wales,* and *North and South Wales.* All in High Street.

Bathing.—Tents and machines, 3*d.* each person. No attendance on Sundays, but the tents and machines are available.

Boating.—6*d.* per hour.

Distances.

	MILES.		MILES.		MILES.
Barmouth	24	Ffestiniog	22	Pont Aberglaslyn	9½
Beddgelert	11	Harlech (by rail)	14	Portmadoc	5
Carnarvon	22	,, (by sea)	7	Pwllheli	8

Hotels.—*See* Introduction.

London Papers arrive about 2.0; Provincial, about 10.0.

Places of Worship, with the hours of English services on Sundays:—
St. Deiniol's, 11.15 and 7.30.
Presbyterian, 11.0 and 7.0.
Wesleyan, 11.0 and 7.0.
Llanystumdwy Church, (1½ miles) first Sunday in the month, at 3 p.m.

Population.—4,700.

Post and Telegraph Office.—High Street. Sub-Postoffice, 1, Marine Crescent.

Sea-fishing.—Mackerel and flat fish can be caught in the sea, and good baskets of prawns can be obtained from the rocks.

Tennis.—Day ticket, 1 6; weekly, 5/-; fortnightly, 8 ; monthly, 12/6; season, 15/. Family season tickets can be obtained at half the ordinary rate.

Criccieth—charming Criccieth—is a town of considerable antiquity. A few of its old cottages still remain, but for the most part its buildings are modern, and chiefly consist of terraces of houses designed for the accommodation of summer visitors. The householders, however, as a rule are not wholly dependent upon the gains of the summer season; consequently the charges are not so high as in places where lodging-house keeping is the chief industry, and the houses have a greater air of comfort. Criccieth embraces characteristics both rural and marine. Its buildings are freely scattered about, and here and there are extensive "greens," which have been planted with shrubs that are both ornamental and useful, seeing that they bear living testimony to the mildness of

The Climate.

Such plants as the myrtle, fuchsia, and hydrangea flourish in the open. Indeed, fuchsias 12 to 15 feet in height may be seen blooming in exposed situations.

Although other watering-places on the Welsh coast have, to some extent, a southern aspect, yet Criccieth is the only one in North Wales which faces *due* south, and as the ground slopes in the same direction, the town gets the full benefit of the sun's rays. In the number of its rainy days, Criccieth compares favourably with south coast resorts. For instance, in 1898, the number of days on which ·01 or more rain fell at Criccieth was 146, about the same as for Torquay (144), Bournemouth (147), and Ventnor (151).

Criccieth is frequently visited by eminent members of the medical profession, many of whom send their patients to it. The facts to which their personal visits point cannot be better expressed than in the words of Dr. Percy Lush, of London, after several visits in the course of four or five years: — " I think that one may fairly say that the number of medical men who visit Criccieth, several of whom represent the most eminent names in the profession, may be taken as evidence that Criccieth is a distinctly healthy place."

The late Dr. J. S. Bristowe, Senior Physician to St. Thomas' Hospital, after three visits of six weeks' duration each, thus wrote of Criccieth: " I regard it as a particularly salubrious locality, and it is one of the places which I have recommended, and shall continue to recommend, to my friends and patients who are in search of health and enjoyment."

The town is well drained, and has a good supply of pure water from springs which flow into a natural reservoir of slate formation.

The history of the town is intimately connected with the annals of

The Ancient Castle,

which occupies a commanding position on a neck of land projecting into the sea, and dividing the beach into two sections. The public are admitted into the Castle grounds on payment of *one penny*.

The rock on which the Castle stands has been fortified from the very earliest times. The founder of the present Castle is unknown. Edward I. strengthened and cased the towers,

and portions of two of these are still standing. The Castle
was occupied down to the time of Queen Elizabeth. It is now
in the possession of Lord Harlech. Much historical information respecting the Castle and the town will be found in the
Official Guide to Criccieth, by T. Burnell, price twopence.

The Beach

is a mixture of sand and pebbles. It is not of great extent.
To the west of the Castle it is bounded by cliffs on which
stands the Marine Terrace; to the east of the Castle an
esplanade has been constructed. The water never recedes
far, and as there are absolutely no currents, safe and pleasant
bathing can be enjoyed at any hour of the day.

The boating, and especially canoeing, is extensively
patronised, and so safe is the pastime here that dozens of
visitors, including ladies and young children, may be seen
upon the water, each paddling his or her own canoe. The
pleasure boats are registered, and the boating is regulated by
the by-laws of the local governing body—the Urban District
Council.

Criccieth has two buildings belonging to

The Established Church.

The **Parish Church** was rebuilt in 1873. In form it resembles
its predecessor. It is a low building, consisting of a small
nave and aisle; is dedicated to St. Catherine, has sitting
accommodation for about 300 persons, and is chiefly used for
services in Welsh.

At a short distance from it stands the new **Church of St.
Deiniol**, of much greater dimensions, and in the Early Decorated style of architecture. The services in it are conducted
in English.

The Castle is

A Good View Point.

Another is a hill which stands between the railway station
and the shore, and over and around which a footpath runs.
There being no neighbouring heights to intercept the view,
an extensive prospect may be enjoyed from the summit. It
includes the sea, with Harlech Castle and Cader Idris rising
over the hills at its back; the coast from Wylfa Head right
down to the confines of South Wales; and landward, quite a

multitude of the everlasting hills. Among the more prominent of these are Snowdon, Moel Hebog, Moelwyn, and the Rivals.

With facilities for

Recreation

apart from the sea Criccieth is well provided. There is a tennis club ground, consisting of eight courts, to which visitors are admitted daily from morning until dusk, except on Tuesdays, when the ground is closed to visitors at 4 o'clock. A short distance from this ground is a cricket field, in which matches are played by visitors. Particulars can be obtained at the Llanystumdwy Rectory.

Concerts and other public entertainments are held in the Parish Hall and the Town Hall.

Golf and angling can be enjoyed, as indicated in the appendices, and cyclists will be interested in the following extract from a leading article in the *Lady's Pictorial* :

"There are several capital watering-places in Wales, where cycling can be enjoyed, and where the rider has the great advantages of good roads and fine scenery at hand, and indeed we are inclined to think the Welsh seaside resorts are in this respect among the best from the cycling point of view. . . . We are inclined to place either the small and little known village of Criccieth, or else Llanfairfechan, at the head of the list. We have worked from both centres."

Closely connected with the cycling runs are the

SHORT WALKS FROM CRICCIETH.

These are a special feature of the place.

1. THE BLACK ROCK AND CAVES.

The Black Rock is on the shore, about a mile eastward of the Castle Hill. It can be reached by walking along the beach, a rough bit of which can be avoided by taking the path by the side of the railway. The entrance to this is at the level crossing.

The caves are in the cliffs immediately beyond the Black Rock, and are best seen at low water. They can be reached by boat, or by a path leading over the hill in which they are situated.

Instead of returning by the beach, the visitor can take the cart track to the left of the Black Rock. This will lead towards **Treflys Church**, which will be seen standing on a hill. The road to the left of that church should be followed. Ynyscynhaiarn Parish Church will be seen in a hollow, and the visitor will be brought to the Portmadoc road, through a gate under the railway bridge at Wern, or by a path leading under the railway.

2. TO EDNYFED HILL.

This is but a very short distance from Criccieth. Its summit is only about 350 feet above sea level, but it commands a very extensive view, which includes Snowdon and Cardigan Bay. The route to it runs past the Parish Church (the old church), along a road which leads through two gates, and almost to the summit.

3. TO LLANYSTUMDWY,

a village about 1½ miles from Criccieth, on the Pwllheli road. It is a very picturesque little place, built in a wooded hollow on the banks of the Dwyfawr, which is crossed by a charming old-world bridge. Several county families have shown their appreciation of the scenery by building seats in the neighbourhood.

Take the first turning on the right westward of the Post Office, and at the top of the lane turn to the left along the Upper road, as it is called, to distinguish it from the main road, which is sometimes called the Lower road. Just before reaching the bridge, turn off into the wood on the right, and go down to the water's edge to enjoy the view along the river. A path runs by the side of the stream to the bridge. Return to Criccieth by the main road; the telegraph wires will guide you.

4. TO RHYDYCROESAU BRIDGE, 2½ miles.

Proceed to Llanystumdwy village as above. Cross the bridge and go along the main road to the top of the hill, and there turn to the right. At the lodge entrance turn to the left. Much of the walk is in the shade of trees, and the scenery is delightful.

The visitor who prefers not to retrace his steps, and does not object to an additional mile, may return to Criccieth by taking the road to the left, on the farther side of Rhydycroesau bridge, and turning to the left again on reaching the main road. This route crosses the Dwyfach at Bontfechan.

5. TO RHYDYBENLLIG BRIDGE.

This is a shady spot, the delight of the angler and the artist. Follow the Carnarvon road for about half a mile, and where a guide-post directs, strike across three fields approached by stone steps. After much rain, parts of the ground are rather boggy.

From the third field, a short lane leads into the high road, in which turn to the left, and the bridge and the old mill on the bank of the river will quickly be reached. For a good view, cross the bridge, turn off to the left, and go down to the bank of the stream.

Taking the route in the reverse direction, on entering the second field, keep to the right along the wall.

The return may be made *viâ* Llanystumdwy.

From Rhydybenllig Bridge, proceed along the Carnarvon road to a cross-road about half a mile from the bridge. There turn to the left. On reaching Llanystumdwy, cross the bridge, and then follow either the upper or the lower road to Criccieth. With this extension the walk will measure about 5 miles.

6.   TO CEFNISA CROMLECH.

Proceed to Rhydybenllig Bridge as above, and to the cross-road half a mile beyond. There turn to the right. In a few yards turn again to the right, in front of a row of cottages, and the cromlech will soon be seen in a field, a short distance from the bridge.

7.   TO YSTUMCEGID CROMLECH.

This is the largest cromlech in the district. It stands about two miles from Criccieth. To reach it, proceed along the Carnarvon road for about a mile. Then take the road to the right, opposite a farmhouse called Gell, which stands on the left-hand side of the road, a few yards from the turning at the top of the hill. Next pass through a white iron gate, and follow the road across which it shuts until a farmhouse is reached on the left. There follow a cart road leading past the house and through two fields (taking care to close all gates which have to be opened). Beyond the second field you come to some farm buildings. These have to be left on the right, and another field has to be entered over stone steps. Then the cromlech will be seen a few yards ahead.

8.   TO THE VALE OF PENNANT,

a romantic spot 6 miles north of Criccieth. Through it flows the upper part of the Dwyfawr. At the upper end are Hebog, Llwyd Mawr, and other mountains of Snowdonia. It is a habitat of rare ferns, including the parsley fern.

To get to it by the shortest route, follow the Carnarvon road for about a mile; take the first by-road on the right; follow it through the white iron gate and as far as Ymwlch Lodge. There pass through a small gate on the left of the lodge, and ascend the hill. At the top go through the farm-yard on the right and pass the back of Ymwlch. The main road will soon be reached. On getting to it, turn to the left, and at Dobennaen Church, about a mile farther, turn to the right, and the road leads straight to Pennant.

Excursions from Criccieth.

There are no public excursions by road direct from Criccieth, but some of the coach excursions from Pwllheli can be conveniently joined, and tickets for the rail-and-road excursions organized by the Cambrian Railways Co. are issued from Criccieth.

Conveyances for private parties can be obtained at Criccieth on very reasonable terms.

Tickets for use on Cycling and Walking Tours and Day Excursion Tickets are also issued every week-day.

Tickets for the Circular Tour by Rail are issued from Criccieth at 5/6 each.

PORTMADOC

is a small but busy place, which has, in itself, little of interest from a tourist's point of view. It is, however, the starting-point of several excursions in connection with the Cambrian Railways Co., particulars of which are given below. It contains a pretty new church (St. John's) and several fine hotels. It has a harbour accessible to vessels of 600 tons burthen, and a considerable trade, principally in slate, brought from Ffestiniog and its neighbourhood. A short walk over the hill at the back of the town affords a splendid view of the coast, and a mile and a half off there is a pretty little seaside village called **Borthy-Gest**, where boating and bathing may be indulged in. The town is, as its name implies, the port of Tremadoc. It is also the terminus of

The Ffestiniog Toy Railway,

a ride along which is always a favourite excursion with tourists.

The railway is a single line of 1 foot 11½ inches gauge (called the two-foot gauge), extending from the port to some slate quarries at Blaenau Ffestiniog and Duffws, in the neighbourhood of Ffestiniog. Its length is 13¼ miles, exclusive of branches about 1¼ miles long, leading to Duffws and Minffordd. The main line rises 700 feet, the gradients being continuous, but variable. The least is 1 in 186, while the steepest are 1 in 68-69, 1 in 50, and 1 in 36 on its branches.

When its construction was commenced in 1832, it was intended that the line should merely be a tramway, which the

CRICCIETH

THE TOY RAILWAY AT TAN-Y-BWLCH

trains of loaded slate wagons should descend by gravity, while the empty trucks were to be hauled back by horses. This plan was adopted, and continued in operation till 1863, when, on the recommendation of Mr. C. E. Spooner, the engineer of the line, locomotive power was employed. During the autumn of 1864, passengers were carried by the company experimentally, without charge, and, in the following year, the line was regularly opened for passenger traffic.

Traversing a rugged but most picturesque tract of country —now creeping along the steep hill-side, hundreds of feet above the valley below; now crossing deep ravines on narrow embankments, or rather walls of dry stone masonry, some of them 60 feet in height; and then again threading its way through cuttings in the rock, only to burst out anew into the open and disclose a fresh panorama to the view—the line presents ever-changing features of interest. Throughout almost its entire course it consists of a series of curves, varying in radius from 28 chains to as little as 1¼ chains, some of the curves of the latter radius being 200 feet in length. There are two tunnels on the line, one 60 yards and the other 730 yards in length. There are, besides the termini, seven intermediate stations on the Ffestiniog Railway. They have no raised platforms (the lowness of the carriages rendering this unnecessary), but they are provided with all requisite accommodation, although on a small scale. It has also an admirable permanent way, with an excellent system of rail fastenings, designed by Mr. C. E. Spooner, and very conducive to easy and safe travelling. The line is worked on the "staff" system, assisted by the telegraph; and the signalling arrangements, systems of points and crossings, turntables, etc., are as complete as possible. There is no night traffic on it, and no Sunday trains are run. The engines are specially designed to meet the steep gradients and curves of the line. The *Little Wonder*, the oldest of these interesting locomotives, was introduced in 1869. It is mounted on two steam bogies, each bogie having four coupled wheels, 2 feet 4 inches in diameter. Each two has a pair of cylinders, 8¼ inches in diameter, with a 13 inch stroke. In ordinary work this engine will take up a train consisting of seven carriages (first, second, and third class), a guard's brake-van, six to ten goods wagons, and 112 empty slate wagons; the total gross weight, inclusive of engine, being about 110 tons. A train of this description measures over 1,200 feet in length, and on some parts of the line it is serpentine on three or more curves at once, the different portions of the train moving towards almost all points of the compass. Riding in one of the last wagons of such a train, it is at times difficult for a stranger to realize the fact that the engine which he sees moving along the contrary side of a ravine, in a direction almost exactly opposite to that in which he is travelling, can possibly have any connection with the vehicle in which he is sitting. The speed was at first limited by Board of Trade regulations; but these restrictions have been removed, and, on portions of the line the engines sometimes run more than 30 miles an hour.

Leaving Portmadoc,

we cross the estuary on which the harbour is constructed, and see the viaduct by which the Cambrian line is carried over it, a little inland.

As far as **Minffordd Junction**, the first station on the line, we ride near the coast; but from this point the course is inland and upward. Near the station we cross the Cambrian Railway, the traffic with which is interchanged here; and leaving it, stop at **Penrhyn** (Penrhyndeudraeth is the full name of the village).

The line runs almost along the brink of a precipice, on the edge of the glen of **Tan-y-Bwlch**, a very beautiful and fashionable resort for families and tourists during the summer season. The hotel (*Oakeley Arms*) is situated on a gentle declivity, in the centre of many attractive objects. Among them is the mansion of *Tan-y-Bwlch*, to the charming grounds of which visitors are allowed access by free tickets, obtained at the hotel. The station is 100 feet above the level of the sea, and is a long mile from the hotel, which, by the way, contains a post and telegraph office. The road to Tal-y-Bwlch hotel goes on to Maentwrog Village and to the Raven and Rhayadr Du Waterfalls.

From the station also two roads lead off on the left to **Beddgelert**. One is a mountain road, by which can be made

The Ascent of Moelwyn.

This mountain is about 4 miles from Tan-y-Bwlch, and over 2,500 feet high. A rough glen introduces the pedestrian to the base of the mountain, which stands amid wild and gloomy surroundings. There is no difficulty in the approach, which is generally a slightly ascending gradient, up a lonely valley. But the hill itself, particularly the upper part, is steep; and owing to the slate *débris* and shale, the ascent is toilsome till the climber is about half-way up. The view is very fine. It is wilder and more solemn than that from Snowdon.

Tan-y-Bwlch is the half-way station. Very shortly after

leaving it, Ffestiniog may be plainly seen on the right-front. Indeed, the finest view of the Vale of Ffestiniog and of the river Dwyryd is obtained before reaching **Dduallt**, the next station.

From Dduallt Station a path leads to the gorge of the Cymmerau and along the Tigel Dingle to the **Cymmerau Falls** and **Roman Bridge**. Thence the road leads past **Dolwen Waterfalls** and Rustic Bridge to Tan-y-Grisiau Station. This route is through one of the most charming pieces of scenery in the district. **Tan-y-Grisiau** Station comes next to that of Dduallt, and is at the end of the best of the scenery. Visitors bound for Ffestiniog will do well to alight here, and pursue the rest of the way on foot.

A very pleasant excursion is to take the train to Tan-y-Grisiau, walk to Ffestiniog, and thence walk back to Dduallt.

The ascent of Moelwyn can also be made from Tan-y-Grisiau. There is an easy route by the road leading past the Cwmorthin lake and the Rhosydd Quarry, and thence by a path to the summit.

Passengers who continue to travel by the train may find themselves somewhat puzzled by the multiplicity of stations near the terminus. The train first arrives at

Blaenau Ffestiniog,

where passengers change for the London and North-Western Railway for Bettws-y-Coed, Llandudno, etc. A short distance farther the train stops at a platform, where those alight who want the Great Western Railway for Ffestiniog, Bala, etc. A little beyond that is **Duffws**, the terminus of the line.

Duffws Station and the other stopping places just named are all in Blaenau Ffestiniog, a place which was called into existence by the slate mines, and contains nothing to detain the tourist.

Blaenau Ffestiniog is one of the places at which tickets are issued every week-day for a circular tour, embracing Portmadoc, Harlech, Barmouth, Dolgelley, Bala, and Ffestiniog. The tickets (3rd class, 5/-) are available on the day of issue and the following day. The journey may be broken at *any* station.

EXCURSIONS BY RAIL AND ROAD FROM PORTMADOC.

Portmadoc is the point at which the railway is left in the course of two excursions organised by the Cambrian Railways Co.

1. **To Beddgelert.** The coach leaves the station after the arrival of the 7.15 a.m. train from Aberystwyth (9.10 from

Barmouth), the 9.50 train from Pwllheli, and the 10.20 from Criccieth. The route, both going and returning, is *viâ* Tremadoc and the Pass of Aberglaslyn. Beddgelert is reached about noon, and the coach leaves at 2.30 p.m. in time for the train at 5.20 from Portmadoc to Criccieth and Pwllheli, and that at 1.52 for other stations.

2. **To Snowdon** *viâ* **Beddgelert and the North Wales Narrow Gauge Railway.** The coach leaves after the arrival of the trains named above, and goes through the Pass of Aberglaslyn to Beddgelert, which is reached at 12.0 noon. After allowing time to view Gelert's grave and to lunch (cold luncheon at *Royal Goat* and *Prince Llewelyn* Hotels, 2/), the coach journey is resumed. The conveyance leaves the *Royal Goat* Hotel at 2.30, and proceeds to Snowdon Station, where passengers are transferred to the *North Wales Narrow Gauge* (2-ft.) *Railway*, on which, in diminutive carriages, they travel to **Dinas Junction,** 12¼ miles from the other end of the line, and 3 miles south of Carnarvon. Dinas Junction is reached in time for the 4.13 train for Pwllheli, Dolgelley, and intermediate stations; but passengers for stations beyond Barmouth must stay the night in that town, and return to their destination by 7.50 a.m. or 12.30 p.m. train on the following day.

The tour can be worked in the reverse direction, viz., by rail *viâ* Afon Wen and Dinas Junction.

Portmadoc is also one of the stations at which, every week-day, tickets (3rd class, 5/) are issued for a circular tour by rail.

Rather less than 4 miles east of Portmadoc is **Penrhyn Deudraeth,** at which the railway is left in the course of the following five excursions.

EXCURSIONS BY RAIL AND ROAD FROM PENRHYN DEUDRAETH.

1. **To Cynicht,** the "Sugar-loaf Mountain." The conveyance leaves on the arrival of the 7.15 a.m. train from Aberystwyth, 9.10 from Barmouth, and 9.50 from Pwllheli, and proceeds to Cynant-y-Park, passing on the way through the beautiful Vale of Llanfrothen, in view of Snowdon, Moel Hebog, etc., and close to the overhanging rocks of Garreghylldrem. It returns at 1.15 p.m., in time for the 5.10 train to Barmouth, Aberystwyth, etc., and for the 6.38 train to Pwllheli, etc.

2. **To Tan-y-Bwlch, Maentwrog, and Waterfalls.** The coach leaves at 10.15 and 11.0 a.m., and returns from Tan-y-Bwlch at 2.20 for Pwllheli, etc., and 5.15 p.m. for places to the south. The outward route is along the south side of the beautiful Vale of Ffestiniog, and time is allowed to visit the Raven Fall and the Black Cataract. The journey is continued through Maentwrog   to the *Oakeley Arms* Hotel, a little beyond the village, where free tickets can be obtained to visit the

beautiful grounds of the mansion of Tan-y-Bwlch. (Cold luncheon at the *Oakeley Arms*, 2/). The return journey is made along the north side of the vale.

3. **To Beddgelert.** The coach leaves on the arrival of the trains named in No. 1.

On the outward journey it goes through the Vale of Llanfrothen, crosses the Aberglaslyn Bridge, and goes through the Pass of Aberglaslyn to Beddgelert, arriving there at 12.0 noon. It leaves at 2.30, in time for train due to leave Portmadoc at 5.20 for Criccieth and Pwllheli, and 4.52 for other stations. The return is by another route along the Glaslyn River, and passes through the town of Tremadoc.

4. **To Snowdon *via* Beddgelert and the North Wales Narrow Gauge Railway.** The coach leaves on the arrival of the 7.15 a.m. train from Aberystwyth (9.10 from Barmouth). Other particulars are identical with those given in connection with the same excursion from Portmadoc.

5. **To the Foot of Snowdon.** The brake leaves immediately on the arrival of the 9.10 a.m. train from Barmouth, the 9.50 from Pwllheli, and the 10.20 from Criccieth. It goes through the Pass of Aberglaslyn, and arrives at Beddgelert at 11.30. It leaves at noon, and proceeds to the foot of Sir Edward Watkin's path to the summit of Snowdon, arriving there at 12.30, and leaving at 1.0 p.m., so as to reach Portmadoc in time for the 6.50 p.m. train to Pwllheli, and the 7.10 to Barmouth and Dolgelley.

FFESTINIOG.

Ffestiniog is a village delightfully situated at the head of a lovely vale. "With a loving wife, a bosom friend, and a good set of books," said Lord Lyttleton, "one might pass an age in this vale and think it a day." The church, a conspicuous feature in any view of the village, is built in the ancient style of English architecture. It stands on the edge of a cliff overlooking the vale. The village is especially interesting to tourists on account of the splendid mountain walks which can be enjoyed in all directions, and there are several waterfalls in the locality worth viewing.

A Good View Point

of the vale as a whole is in a field entered through a gate to the south-east of the churchyard.

WALKS FROM FFESTINIOG.

1. TO THE CYNFAEL WATERFALLS.

These are only about half a mile distant. One is 300 yards above, and the other is as far below a small bridge. The upper fall consists of three steep rocks, over which the water foams into a deep basin, overshadowed by the adjoining precipices. The other is formed by a bright sheet of water, falling over a slightly shelving rock, about 40 feet high. After the water has reached the bottom of the deep cavity, it rushes along a narrow rocky chasm, when, rolling amid the shaggy rocks, it glistens among the scattered fragments, and falling from slope to slope, gains another smooth bed, and steals away among the mazes of the vale.

Between the lower cataract and the bridge is a tall columnar rock, which stands in the bed of the river. It is called

Hugh Lloyd's Pulpit

because of the tradition that Hugh Lloyd, a reputed magician of the time of James I., used it as a rostrum from which to deliver his incantations.

Not far beyond this the path crosses the stream, and by continuing up it, the visitor presently comes to the view point called

The Goat's Bridge,

a slab connecting the bank with a large, flat-topped boulder in the bed of the stream. Fifty yards farther is a view point of the Higher Fall.

2. TO BEDDAU GWYR ARDUDWY

(" The Tombs of the Men of Ardudwy "). Follow the Bala road for about 2 miles, and then turn up Sarn Helen, an old Roman road, on the left. The site of the tombs is about half a mile from the main road. The tombs consisted of between twenty and thirty oblong mounds, from two to three feet high, every one having a small stone at each end. Tradition affirms that they were the graves of " warriors bold," who, emulating the conduct of the Romans of old, made an incursion into Denbighshire, and vanquishing the men, forcibly tore the women from their families, and returned with them in triumph to their own country. Like the Sabines, the men of Denbighshire resolved on vengeance, and, following " the spoil-encumbered enemy," overtook them at this spot, where they " fought and conquered," defeating the men of Ardudwy with great slaughter. But the encounter had a still more tragic result. The infatuated women had conceived so extraordinary a passion for their abductors that, rather than survive their loss, they drowned themselves in a lake, still known as **Llyn-y-Morwynion** (" Pool of the Maidens ").

3. TO THE RHAIADR-CWM.

This is the name of cataracts 3½ miles from Ffestiniog, along the Bala road. They can also be reached by foot-path *via* Pont Newydd, which is 1¼ miles from Ffestiniog.

4. TO TOMEN-Y-MUR, 3¼ miles.

Proceed to Maentwrog Road Station, on the Great Western line. Thence follow the road for about a quarter of a mile to a schoolhouse, where turn to the left, and then take the second cart road on the left (about 350 yards from the previous turning), and in a few minutes you see Tomen-y-Mur, a Roman or British mound, about 25 feet high, on a grassy knoll behind a farmstead. From it there is a very wide prospect.

5. TO RHAIADR DU AND THE RAVEN FALL.

The former (the Cataract Fall) is 6¼ miles and the latter 6½ miles from Ffestiniog.

Proceed to the schoolhouse mentioned above, and there take the road to Maentwrog Village. At the end of about a quarter of a mile turn to the left ; half a mile farther, to the right ; and then, after a short quarter of a mile, keep to the left again. A short half-mile from the last turning brings you to a cottage and to a steep descent to the glen, in which the falls are situated. After descending for a short distance, pass through a door in a wall on the left, and go a few steps down through a wood ; you then come to a track which, by following to the left, leads up to Rhaiadr Du, a most charming scene.

The Raven Fall is a short distance lower down the glen. The surrounding scenery is very delightful, but the fall is not particularly remarkable.

To make the trip circular from the fall, regain the track which was left to reach the doorway in the wall, descend along it towards the west, and in less than half a mile you strike the high road a mile south-west of

Maentwrog

(*man-too-rog*), a village 3 miles from Ffestiniog, and situated in the most romantic part of the highly picturesque vale. (It is only half a mile from the Tan-y-Bwlch Hotel, p. 161). It derives its name from a large stone in the churchyard, called Maen Twrog (" the Stone of Twrog "). Twrog is said to have been a British saint who died about the year 610.

The present church was built on the site of the ancient structure in 1811.

The Rev. Edmund Prys, one of the most eminent Welsh poets of his time, was rector of this parish. He was the author of the metrical psalms used in the Welsh churches, and also assisted Bishop Morgan in translating the Bible into Welsh. He died in the year 1623, and was buried in Maentwrog Church.

From Maentwrog, a walk of 1½ miles will take you to Tan-y-Bwlch Station, from which you can return to Ffestiniog by rail, *via* Blaenau Ffestiniog. But the better way is to follow the high road to Ffestiniog, which is only 3 miles from Maentwrog.

CARNARVON.

Population. 9,804 (1891).

Post Office.—The Castle Square.

Public Free Library.—Bangor Street.

Steamboats.—Daily to and from Liverpool and Llandudno and the piers in the Menai Straits. Full particulars will be sent on application to the Secretary, the Liverpool and North Wales S.S. Co., Water Street, Liverpool, or to the Company's agent, Carnarvon.

Telephone Call Office.—The Post Office.

Carnarvon, 23¾ miles from Pwllheli, and one less from Criccieth, stands just within the western entrance of the Menai Straits, at the mouth of the river Seiont, and for many centuries was a place of great importance. It is in the midst of pretty scenery, and is annually visited by thousands of persons, who are mainly attracted to it by

The Castle,

which, with the exception of that at Alnwick, in Northumberland, is "the finest castle in Great Britain." It belongs to the Crown, and *visitors are admitted on payment of four-pence each*; but the exterior is much more picturesque than the interior, the south-west side being particularly fine.

The Castle is half a mile from the railway station, from which it is approached by turning to the right and keeping straight on to Castle Square, where the castle will be seen on the right. The walls enclose an area of about 3 acres, and are from 7 to 9 ft. thick. The erection of the fortress was begun by Edward I. in 1283, and was completed by his son. It was twice unsuccessfully besieged by Owen Glyndwr. During the Civil War it was garrisoned for the king, and after changing hands more than once, was finally captured by the forces of the Parliament in 1646. In 1660 a warrant was issued for its demolition, but happily the order was never executed.

The entrance is at the **King's Gate**, beneath a beautiful and lofty archway, over which is a statue of Edward I. or Edward II. On each side of the archway are the grooves of the portcullises. In the towers flanking the gateway are the guardrooms and other apartments, while over the archway are an oratory and a small room used in raising and lowering the drawbridge.

In the courtyard are the remains of the **Banqueting Hall**, which was 100 ft. long, 45 ft. broad, and about 50 ft. high. The kitchens were on the opposite side. The **Well Tower**, so called because it covered the well which supplied the castle with water, was partly rebuilt in 1893–4.

Guarding the mouth of the Seiont is a massive pentagonal tower, called the **Eagle Tower**, through having upon it the figure of an eagle, said by some to have been brought from the ruins of the neighbouring Roman station of Segontium ; but an eagle was one of Edward's crests. This majestic tower rises to the height of 124 ft., has three fine turrets, and its battlements display a mutilated series of heads, wearing armour of the time of Edward II. Access to the summit is gained by 158 stone steps, and a splendid view is obtained therefrom. In the lower part of the tower is shown a small dark room, measuring 12 ft. by 8 ft., in which Edward II. is said to have been born. This tradition, however, is without foundation in fact, for Edward II. had been king nine years before the tower was roofed in. The little apartment contains a stained-glass window, exhibiting the Prince of Wales's feathers.

By keeping to the right from the Eagle Tower, we come to the **Queen's Tower**, now used by the Freemasons. A door close to the curtain-wall gives access to a passage that leads to a corridor, the windows of which opened into the Banqueting Hall. This corridor leads to the Chamberlain's Tower. Coming into the courtyard and re-entering the Chamberlain's Tower by another door, we reach the Black Tower, which contains the smallest rooms in the castle, and was probably the prison. From this tower we go to the entrance on the east side, called the Queen's Gate, because Queen Eleanor is said by tradition to have entered the castle by it.

The Walls,

which formerly enclosed the whole town, are still nearly entire, and a beautiful view may be obtained from their seaward portion. They are flanked with round towers, and had originally two principal gates, others having been added at different times as convenience required. The circuit of the walls can conveniently be begun by turning to the right on leaving the castle. In this way we are led past the river front of the fortress, and beyond the Eagle Tower reach a promenade running at the foot of the western wall, the towers along which house various institutions. Near the north-western angle is the Town Church, or St. Mary's, built partly through the wall. By following the wall, we are led to our starting-point.

The remains of

The Roman City of Segontium,

of which Carnarvon is the modern representative, are of great interest to antiquaries. A short half-mile from the square is Segontium Road. In it, on the left, is a portion of the Roman wall, at right angles to the thoroughfare. A fragment of the wall, now forming the back of a workshop, can be seen, by permission of the occupier, on the Beddgelert Road, a little short of Llanbeblig Church.

Twt Hill,

a rocky eminence, overlooking the town, should be ascended for the sake of the grand panorama which it unfolds. Although the topmost point is only 192 ft. above the sea, the view embraces, in addition to the town and castle, the Menai Strait, a great part of Anglesey, and the great mountain range extending from Penmaenmawr in the north-east to the Rivals in the south-west, a distance of about 35 miles. The hill is near the station, and is approached from the Bangor road by a lane, a few yards on the townward side of the Royal Hotel. By the side of the lane is an immense Eisteddfod Pavilion, capable of seating 7,000 persons.

A four-horse coach leaves Carnarvon daily for

THE LOOP TOUR ROUND SNOWDON,

in connection with the London and North-Western Railway
Company. Passengers have the option of breaking their
journey at Carnarvon, and proceeding within three days by
coach or rail.

This is one of the finest coaching tours that can be enjoyed
in Wales, the route being through the most picturesque
mountain scenery in the Principality. The distance covered
by the coach is 35 miles.

The following time-table is given for the general information of the reader, but should not be implicitly relied upon.

Train arrives from Pwllheli, Criccieth, etc., *via* Afon Wen, 8.21 a.m.
Coach leaves, 10.15 a.m.; arrives at Beddgelert, 12.30 p.m.; departs, 1.45
p.m.; arrives at Llanberis about 4.30 p.m.; departs, 5.0 p.m.; arrives at
Carnarvon, 6.0 p.m. Train leaves, 8.25 p.m.; arrives at Pwllheli, 9.50 p.m.;
Criccieth, 9.38 p.m.; Portmadoc, 9.50 p.m.

FROM CARNARVON TO BEDDGELERT.

The coach starts from the Carnarvon Railway Station, and
calls at the Royal Hotel close by. On its way through the
town the passengers are afforded a good view of the ancient
castle, and of the adjacent square, with its fountain, erected
as a memorial of the opening of the waterworks, and of the
statue of Sir Hugh Owen, "born 1844; died 1881."

Half a mile from the town the coach passes **Llanbeblig Old
Church**, which stands on the site of the city of Segontium,
and is famed for its stepped battlements. Thence the route
is, for a time, through open country, and the village of
Waenfawr is reached some 4 miles from Carnarvon. Here
the road crosses the River Gwyrfai and the North Wales
Narrow Gauge Line, and then keeps close to them for
several miles. The river, by the way, is a good stream for
angling.

About a mile beyond Waenfawr is the village of **Bettws-
Garmon**, which has some claim to be considered picturesque,
especially where an old three-arched bridge crosses the
stream. Another mile brings us abreast of the ruin of **Nant
Mill**, with its equally interesting accessories of waterfall and
bridge, of which one of Cox's *chefs d'œuvre* was a representa-
tion. Cox's painting, though probably disposed of by him
for considerably under £100, changed owners only a few
years ago for more than £1,000.

Continuing our journey, we soon come in sight of **Llyn**

Quellyn, 1½ miles in length, and about half a mile broad. It affords good sport to the angler, who will find comfortable quarters at the *Snowdon Ranger Hotel*, which is close to Quellyn Lake Station (formerly Snowdon Ranger Station). A well known path leads from the hotel to the top of Snowdon. On the opposite side of the lake is **Mynydd Mawr** (the Great Mountain). One of the cliffs, called Carn Cwm Bychan, rises perpendicularly from the water for several hundred feet, to where it presents the appearance of a fortification. The crown of the cliff is called Castell Cidwm (the Wolf's Castle), and tradition says it was the stronghold of a robber chief, who was known as "The Wolf," on account of his murderous propensities and thievish habits. As we skirt the lake the road ascends, and in clear weather Snowdon is revealed in all its glory on the left front.

A mile beyond the lake we reach the wayside village of **Rhyd-ddu**, consisting almost entirely of quarrymen's cottages and an inn. It is the site of a station, formerly named after the village, but now known as "Snowdon," on the narrow-gauge railway, and is within 3½ miles of the summit of Snowdon, the path to which may be almost wholly seen. (Refreshment room at Snowdon Station.)

Soon after leaving the village, we attain the highest point (661 ft. above sea-level) on this portion of the route, and about a mile from the station pass, by the roadside, an isolated mass of rock, which bears so remarkable a resemblance to the profile of William Pitt that it has received the name of Pitt's Head. Near it begins the Beddgelert ascent of Snowdon.

Proceeding for another 3 miles, with the river Colwyn as our companion, we arrive at

BEDDGELERT.

Distances. Snowdon Station, 4 miles ; Bettws-y-Coed, 17½ ; Portmadoc, 8 ; Carnarvon, 13.

London Papers arrive about 2.15 p.m. ; Provincial, 11 a.m.

The site of this village is in the midst of a beautiful tract of meadows, at the junction of three vales, near the confluence of the Glaslyn and the Colwyn, and amid lofty mountains, woods and murmuring streams. It possesses two

features of great interest, apart from the attractive character
of the scenery by which it is surrounded. One is its *Church*,
in the Early Pointed style, which was, in the days long since
gone by, attached to a Priory of Augustinian canons, a resting-place for pilgrims in their journeys to and from Ireland.
The Manor House near the church is supposed to have been
the residence of the prior. The other feature of the place is
the **Tomb of Gelert**, Llewelyn's faithful dog, from which the
place is said to have received its name.

We all know the legend. Gelert, a hound presented to
Llewelyn by King John, stayed at home one day while the
prince and his train were hunting. On his master's return
the dog ran joyfully to meet him, wagging his tail, but
covered with blood. The prince, being alarmed, hastened to
the nursery, and found the cradle in which the child had
lain overturned and the ground stained with blood. Imagin-
ing that the greyhound had killed the child, he immediately
drew his sword and slew him; but on turning up the cradle,
he found the child alive under it.

It seems almost cruel to spoil such a pretty story, but that
must be done if the truth is to be told. Forty years ago a
writer in a Welsh magazine showed that the legend was not
founded on fact, and the Rev. A. Elvet Lewis, in a work
published in 1899, entitled *Bedd Gelert: Its Facts, Fairies,
and Folk-lore*, gives wider publicity to its origin. He shows
that the story, so far as it has local colour, is a growth
of the 19th century; that before 1798 it was unknown in
the neighbourhood; and that it was, in all probability,
imported from South Wales by a certain David Prichard,
who migrated north and became the first landlord of the
Royal Goat Hotel at Beddgelert. Prichard came stocked
with good stories from the south, and among them with that
of "the man who killed his greyhound." He it was who
fitted this particular folk-tale to the scene, and the dog to
the name Gelert; he who told the story to Spencer, the
author of the familiar ballad; and he who, with the artistic
completeness of the born myth-maker, aided by the parish
clerk and another, raised the stone now exhibited on the spot
known as the grave.

Beddgelert is the centre for many charming walks, of
which the chief is that past Gelert's Grave and along the
river to Pont Aberglaslyn. The route lies through the
beautiful **Pass of Aberglaslyn**, on the road to Tremadoc, for
about 1½ miles, the path being bounded on each side by
mountains of great height. The bridge, a single-arched,
ivy-clad structure, is ascribed to Satanic agency. The sur-

rounding scenery can rightly be described as sub-Alpine in character.

Near Beddgelert, on the west side, is **Moel Hebog** (the Hill of the Hawk), where Owen Glyndwr hid himself when pursued by the English. The ascent commences close to the Goat Hotel. It is 2,566 feet in height, and the summit can be reached from Beddgelert in from an hour and a half to two hours.

Coaches run several times a day to Snowdon Station, fare 1 , single ; 1/6, return ; and to Portmadoc, single fare, 2 ; return, 3/ . Every week-day there is a coach to Pen-y-Gwryd, fare 2/6 ; to Llanberis, fare 5 ; to Capel Curig, fare 4/ ; and to Bettws-y-Coed, fare 5/ . Particulars of circular tours, which include Beddgelert, will be found in the London and North Western Railway Company's Programme of Coach Tours, and in the Time-bills of the North Wales Narrow Gauge Railway.

BEDDGELERT TO LLANBERIS.

Leaving the Royal Goat Hotel, we once more pass over the Colwyn, and, proceeding to the right, soon begin to ascend a most lovely valley to Pen-y-Gwryd. On each side of the

road are high, precipitous mountains, and the Glaslyn
dashes down the valley. In front is seen the summit of **Moel
Siabod**, and on the left is **Arran**, one of the peaks of Snowdon. We pass, at a distance, a wooded eminence called
Dinas Emrys, to which, legend says, Vortigern retired and
Merlin came to his aid. Then, less than 2 miles from
Beddgelert, we reach **Llyn-y-Ddinas**, a small but beautiful
lake, from one end of which is a fine view of Moel Hebog.
A little farther along the road we have a glimpse of the
summit of Snowdon. After crossing the Glaslyn, we keep
up **Nant Gwynant** until we reach the beautiful lake of that
name, four miles from Beddgelert. Rising out of the water
is Gallt-y-Wenallt, a rocky shoulder of Snowdon. We skirt
the lake, which is about a mile in length, and then, proceeding uphill for nearly another 3 miles, through most attractive scenery, we reach the *Pen-y-Gwryd Hotel*, about 7½ miles
from Beddgelert. It is the only house in the locality. Its
site is 907 feet above sea-level, at the junction of the road
by which we have travelled with the Pass of Llanberis and
the road to Capel Curig. In the immediate vicinity of the
house is one of the routes to the summit of Snowdon. It
may be remembered that the hotel is mentioned in Kingsley's
Two Years Ago. On one occasion the novelist, accompanied
by Tom Taylor and the author of *Tom Brown's Schooldays*,
stayed at the house. The three friends amused themselves
by writing some oft-quoted hybrid verses in the Visitors'
Book. Unfortunately, the pages they used have been stolen.

From Pen-y-Gwryd the route takes a fresh direction,
but continues on the rise for another mile. It bends round
Y Foel-berfedd, a "cub" of Glyder-fawr, and then takes a
north-westerly direction, which it maintains for about 10
miles. A mile from Pen-y-Gwryd we reach a level spot
appropriately named **Gorphwysfa**, "the resting-place," but
more frequently called Pen-y-Pass. Here stands a hotel.
Its site is 1,179 feet above the sea.

From "the resting-place" we begin the descent of the
celebrated **Pass of Llanberis**, which may, without exaggera-
tion, be described as the finest carriage mountain road in
Wales. The precipitous and craggy sides of the noble
mountains press closely on each other and shut in the narrow pass. Shattered masses of every form, which have been
hurled down from the heights, are lying about in strange

confusion, and amidst them the Seiont, rushing and roaring, hastens its descent to the head of Llyn Peris. Tourists descending the pass should look for the train of the Snowdon Mountain Tramroad on the ridge of the mountain above Cwm Glas.

About 1½ miles from the Gorphwysfa Hotel, on the right-hand side of the road, is an enormous fragment of rock that has fallen from the side of Glyder-fawr. It is popularly called the *Cromlech Stone*. Resting upon other fragments, it leaves a cavity beneath, which an old woman named Hetty was wont to occupy.

Some 2 miles farther we reach the picturesque village of **Old Llanberis**, which has a Church worthy of a visit; and soon afterwards we are running by the side of Llyn Peris, on the opposite shore of which are the huge Dinorwic slate-quarries. Then, passing the remains of **Dolbadarn Castle**, we arrive by a park-like approach at the *Royal Victoria Hotel* in modern Llanberis.

At the foot of the hotel lies the lower terminus of the mountain tram-road. Passengers may here break their journey, if they so desire, and go up Snowdon and then take train at Llanberis for their journey home. No extra charge or abatement is made for this break.

LLANBERIS.

Dark Room for Photographers.—Iden House Temperance Hotel.

Distances. *By rail.*

	MILES.		MILES.		MILES.
Carnarvon	9	Llandudno	36	London	257

By road.

	MILES.		MILES.		MILES.
Bettws-y-Coed		Beddgelert	14½	Pen-y-Gwryd	6½
Station	16¼	Capel Curig	10½	Portmadoc	22

By Llanberis is meant the modern village which bears that name. It contains the railway station, and is a good 2 miles from the old village. It is a common centre of the coach routes from Bettws-y-Coed, Bangor, Carnarvon, and Beddgelert, and the headquarters chosen by the great majority of tourists who make the ascent of Snowdon, the Glyders, the Elidirs, and Moel Eilio. The village is situated on the western side of **Llyn Padarn**, which is 2 miles long, and so narrow as to present more the appearance of a river than that of a lake. It is connected with **Llyn Peris** by the river

BEDDGELERT

LLANBERIS LAKE

THE ASCENT OF SNOWDON

Seiont. Boating can be enjoyed on Llyn Padarn and Llyn Peris. Both lakes and the river afford sport for the angler, but the fishing in the upper lake, Llyn Peris, is the property of the Snowdon Tramroad and Hotel Company. It is free to visitors at the Company's hotels—Victoria and Padarn Villa. At the end of Llyn Padarn is a picturesque stone bridge leading to a Roman camp, at Dinas Dinorwic, about a mile off. About 200 yds. from the Victoria Hotel, where the key is kept, are the remains of **Dolbadarn Castle**. They consist only of a round tower, which probably does not date back many centuries, but the site is said to have been held by the Prince of North Wales in the 6th century.

Half a mile south from the Castle is the Fall of Ceunant Mawr, the height of which exceeds 60 ft., but it is only effective after heavy rain.

Coaches from Llanberis. Every week-day to Bettws-y-Coed, 5s.; Beddgelert, 5s.; Portmadoc, 7s., and Carnarvon.

LLANBERIS TO CARNARVON.

There is nothing calling for special notice on this portion of the route. Just beyond Llyn Padarn we pass through Cwmyglo, and then through a rugged-looking, poorly cultivated tract to Pontrug, 3½ miles short of Carnarvon. The city is entered on the side opposite that from which the departure was made.

THE ASCENT OF SNOWDON.

Snowdon is the highest and finest mountain in the southern portion of Great Britain. It has five distinct peaks, viz., Yr Aran, Lliwedd, Crib-y-Ddysgyl, Crib-goch, and Y Wyddfa. The last-named is the central and loftiest. It is 3,560 feet above sea-level. As close as possible to the highest ground is the upper terminus of the mountain tramroad, while the limited area of the very summit is the site of a cairn erected by the ordnance surveyors, and of a neat hotel owned and managed by the Tramroad Company. The apartments include ten bedrooms and two large refreshment rooms, each capable of accommodating some 70 or 80 persons. The eatables are prepared at one of the Company's hotels at the foot of the mountain, and are supplied at very reasonable charges. (For Tariff—*see* Introduction.) At the summit station of the Mountain Railway is a telegraph office (12 words for sixpence), and picture post cards can be obtained. There is also telephonic communication for the use of visitors only, between the Summit Hotel and the Victoria and Padarn Villa Hotels, Llanberis (30 words for threepence).

Each morning a report of the weather at the summit is exhibited in the railway stations at the tourists' resorts.

Every week-day during the summer season, except bankholiday, excursion tickets, available by certain trains, are issued from the principal railway stations in the district. For a slight additional payment the tickets may be used both at Llanberis and at Snowdon station on the North Wales Narrow-Gauge line, so that the holders may ascend by one path and descend by another.

There are five well-beaten tracks to the summit, all free from danger, and in addition there is

The Mountain Tramroad.

Fares.—Return, 5s.; Single up, 3s. 6d.; Single down, 2s. 6d.

The lower terminal station is about five minutes' walk from the London and North-Western Station at Llanberis.

The length of the line is 4¾ miles. The track has been laid on the solid all the way. The gauge is 2 ft. 7½ in. The rails are of the ordinary pattern, and are firmly bolted to steel sleepers, which are hollowed underneath so that they may be firmly embedded.

The mechanism for propulsion consists of a double steel rack, firmly bolted to the centre of the line, and in the deeply-cut indentation of the rack the driving pinions of the engines work. There are four of these pinions, which are very massive, and continually in gear; and the whole power of the engine being available for braking purposes, the train can be brought to a dead stand instantly. As an additional precaution extra lip girders have been provided under which powerful brackets run, so that it is absolutely impossible for the engine or carriages to mount the rack without pulling up the rails and sleepers. The carriages have separate brakes, and during the ascent and descent the engine is at the lower end of the train.

The route has been selected so as to cause as little disfigurement to the mountain as possible, and at the same time to enable passengers to see what is best worth seeing on Snowdon. Soon after leaving the Llanberis terminus, a fine viaduct of fourteen arches affords a full view of the Great Waterfall. Then, after passing the first of the three intervening stations, the line ascends along the east side of Cwm Brwynog until the ridge overlooking the pass is

THE PASS OF LLANBERIS

THE UPPER LAKE, LLANBERIS, AND SNOWDON

reached. From this point the view becomes grander and more extensive at every yard.

The trains run at frequent intervals. The time occupied in ascending or descending is seventy minutes.

1. The Path from Llanberis.

This is the easiest route for pedestrians, and on that account is the most generally chosen. It is, indeed, so comparatively easy and gradual that ponies can be taken all the way, and carts for the greater part of the distance. Unfortunately it is the least interesting. Its length is just under 5 miles, and may be accomplished in about three hours. To get to the path from the station, follow the main road to the Victoria Hotel, and then take a lane on the right. This soon reaches a wood, which is entered by a gate. Follow the cart-track through the wood. Just after leaving the wood it turns sharply to the left, and thence is perfectly plain. At the end of a short half-hour's walk from the wood stands a cottage on the left. At a height of 1,450 feet, about 2¼ miles from Llanberis, the path passes under the tramroad. About a mile farther is a refreshment hut, generally called the *Halfway House*. Thence the track is steeper. At the height of 2,750 feet the path again passes under the tramroad, and a fine view is afforded of the Llanberis Pass and Cwm Glas Bach, which lie immediately below. A little higher is a small spring, and in the vicinity the path receives the Snowdon Ranger route on the right and the Capel Curig route on the left. The elevation of this spot is about 3,260 feet, and a steep climb for about a quarter of an hour completes the ascent.

2. The Snowdon Ranger (Quellyn Lake Station) Route.

The distance by this route is about 4 miles, and will occupy a couple of hours. The path commands fine views, but is very soft after rain. The ascent begins near the Quellyn Lake Station on the North Wales Narrow-Gauge Railway, which joins the London and North-Western line at Dinas Junction, 3 miles south of Carnarvon. Near the lower end of the path is a farmhouse, soon after passing which the path has a zigzag course, and leads through a gate. At the end of half an hour's walk there is another gate and the path becoming indistinct, the left shoulder of Snowdon must be taken as a guide, until the track again appears. It finally crosses the tramroad and joins the Llanberis path near the junction of that route with the path from Pen-y-Gwryd.

The following facts may be noted by those making the *descent* by this path. The Quellyn Lake or Snowdon

Ranger Hotel is situated in a clump of trees about the middle of the eastern side of the lake, and is visible from the

SNOWDON, FROM THE PINNACLES

top of Snowdon. The path leaves the Llanberis route a short half-mile from the summit.

3. From Beddgelert or Snowdon Station.

The distance to the summit from Beddgelert is 6½ miles; from Snowdon Station it is 3½ miles. The paths unite about three-quarters of a mile from the high road. The ascent from the station will occupy a good two hours. Snowdon Station is on the narrow-gauge line mentioned above. From Beddgelert follow the Carnarvon road for about 2¾ miles, and there, just short of the Pitt's Head Rock, pass from the road to the right through a farm.

From Snowdon Station the summit of the mountain is in full view, and far up on a shoulder of the mountain may be seen a wall through which the path runs. Less than halfway up, at the foot of a steep and rocky portion of the route is a capital refreshment room. At the elevation of 3,080 feet the path runs along the ridge of Bwlch-y-Maen, some seven or eight feet wide. The uppermost portion of the route is very steep and rocky, but is perfectly safe.

We would advise those who go to and from Snowdon by train to ascend by the Llanberis path and descend to Snowdon Station.

The descent begins close to the railway station, and the track is unmistakable. In three-quarters of a mile it swerves to the right, and runs along the ridge of Llechog, near the end of which it passes through a wall and presently goes through the wall again. Then it passes some sheep-pens, and becomes indistinct. Hereabouts it bends to the right and crosses a field to a gate by a sheepfold, beyond which it winds among the rocks until it reaches a green road. Pedestrians bound for Beddgelert cross this road, but those making for Snowdon Station follow the road to the right.

4. Sir Edward Watkin's Path.

This lies beyond the route just described. By it the summit is 7½ miles from Beddgelert and 4½ miles from the high-road. The path leaves the high-road between Llyn Dinas and Llyn Gwynant and passes through the grounds of Sir Edward Watkin's house. The route is easy until some slate quarries are reached. There the path made by Sir Edward Watkin begins, and is too plain to be missed. It should be ascended rather than descended.

5. The Capel Curig Route.

This is the wildest and grandest of the approaches to the summit of Snowdon. It should only be attempted in clear, settled weather. From Capel Curig the distance to the top is 9 miles, from Pen-y-Gwryd 5 miles, and Corph-

wysfa Hotel 1 miles. Pen-y-Gwryd and Corphwysfa (Pen-y-Pass) are on the high-road from Capel Curig
to Llanberis. The time occupied in making the ascent from
either will be from two to three hours. A pony can be
taken all the way, although the upper part is exceedingly
steep. The high-road is left near the hotel at Corphwysfa.
The path is passable for vehicles for the first 2 miles. At
the end of about a mile it reaches Llyn Teyrn, a small lake
in a hollow. Another half-mile or so brings it to Llyn
Llydaw, a sheet of water more than a mile long. Instead
of going the length of the lake along its southern side, the

THE SUMMIT OF SNOWDON

pedestrian can cut off a corner, unless there has been much
rain, by crossing the lake by a causeway near the eastern end,
and then following the path along the northern shore.
From Llyn Llydaw, 1,420 feet above sea-level, there is a
steep ascent to Llyn Glaslyn at an elevation of 1,975 feet.
In the vicinity of the latter lake are old copper mines, and
there the cart-track ceases. It is succeeded by a rough and
steep zigzag path, which, in clear weather, cannot easily
be missed.

Formerly there was an alternative track called the Capel
Curig Upper Path. Of late years it has been neglected, and

is now hardly distinguishable from the neighbouring sheep-tracks. It branched off from the path just described at the end of about a quarter of a mile, and joined it again just beyond Llyn Glaslyn.

To descend by the Capel Curig route, follow the Llanberis path for about a third of a mile. Do not attempt short cuts on the zigzag path, or you may come to grief in a disused mine. The greater part of the route is visible from the summit.

The View from the Summit.

When the conditions are favourable, the prospect is beautiful and extensive. Not the least of the grandeur displayed lies immediately underneath in the appearance presented by the cwms and precipices of Snowdon itself. In exceptionally clear weather the outline of the Cumberland mountains, the Isle of Man, and the Wicklow mountains in Ireland are visible. More frequently almost every conspicuous height in Wales can be distinguished. The course of the Menai Straits can be traced, as can also the coast of South Anglesey, as far as Holyhead mountain some 32 miles distant.

To those unaccustomed to view objects from such a standpoint, nothing, perhaps, is more surprising and interesting than the deceptiveness of the idea of distance. On the west side of Snowdon is an oblong-shaped pool that looks but a third of a mile away, while in reality the distance is 1¼ miles. The church at Llanberis is 4 miles as the crow flies, but appears to be not more than half as far. Llyn Llydaw is apparently so close that one might almost jump into it, but a horizontal line from the summit of Snowdon to a point over the nearest end of the lake would measure nearly a mile.

Taking advantage of the accommodation provided at the top of the mountain by the Tramroad and Hotels Co., many persons remain all night on the summit to enjoy the view at sunrise and sunset.

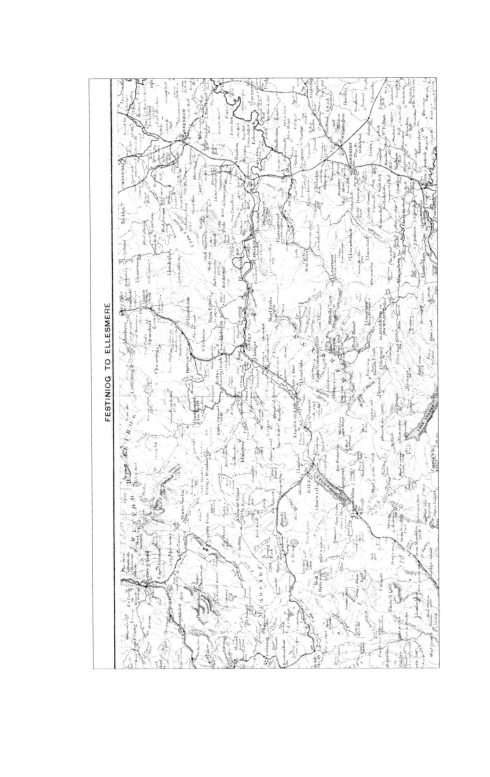

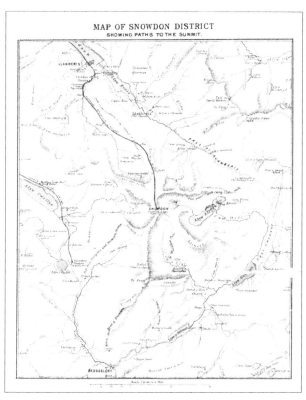

MAP OF SNOWDON DISTRICT
SHOWING PATHS TO THE SUMMIT.

Caernarfon Harbour

Caernarfon Castle (above and below)

Caernarfon (above and below)

A Blaenau Ffestiniog slate quarry

A slate cavern at Blaenau Ffestiniog

A slate cavern at Blaenau Ffestiniog

Ladies in traditional Welsh dress, Llanberis

Llanberis High Street

A slate quarry velocipede, Llanberis

Snowdon from Llanberis quarries

Snowdon Mountain Railway, Llanberis

Slate being loaded onto a sailing ship at Portmadog

Climbing Snowdon

Approaching the Summit of Snowdon

The Summit

A mine on Snowdon

The Summit (above and below)

The easiest way to the Summit

Snowdon Mountain Railway locomotives

The Magic Lantern

The magic lantern was the predecessor of the pre-digital slide projector. The first magic lanterns were made in the mid-1600s by natural philosophers (early scientists) who were exploring the nature and commercial potential of optics. Light sources and lenses improved throughout the 1700s and 1800s and, as a consequence, it was possible to show bigger, brighter and clearer pictures to ever larger audiences. During Queen Victoria's reign, magic lantern shows became established as mass-media entertainment. Shows could be lavish, theatrical events with all the razzmatazz of today's TV talent contests, with multiple lanterns to produce special effects. Magic lanterns were also used in Church and village halls and educational establishments for talks and lectures and, of course, in ordinary homes for family entertainment.

Some slides gave the illusion of movement. These included colourful kaleidoscopes, children skipping, a dentist pulling teeth and a man swallowing rats as he sleeps with his mouth open ...... still a favourite with children (of all ages) who attend my magic lantern shows.

In the early 1800s, magic lanterns were used to create phantasmagoria horror shows, where terrifying devils, witches and the grim reaper were conjured out of thin air, with accompanying sound effects, in suitably scary venues. These shows employed the latest technology and created sophisticated illusions to entice customers to part with their money and be scared out of their wits.

Magic lantern slides were made of glass. Early ones were hand painted and expensive to produce and buy but, from the mid-1800s, photographic images were applied to slides, mass-production followed and the magic lantern industry boomed. In its heyday, the 1890s, millions of slides were made, particularly in Britain, France and America, for entertainment, amusement, education, spiritual enlightenment and moral crusades.

In Britain, lantern slides could be purchased or hired by mail-order direct from the manufacturers or from local, high-street outlets. Photographic slides produced by the best Victorian photographers, such as those reproduced in this booklet, have pin-sharp clarity and can still make an audience gasp in surprise and delight when shown as part of my Victorian magic lantern shows.

Andrew Gill: I have collected historical photographs and optical antiques for over forty years. I am a professional 'magic lantern' showman presenting Victorian slide shows and giving talks on early optical entertainments for museums, festivals, special interest groups and universities. Please visit my website '**Magic Lantern World'** at www.magiclanternist.com

My booklets and photo albums are available from Amazon, simply search for the titles below. If you've enjoyed this book, please leave a review on Amazon, as good ratings are very important to independent authors. If you're disappointed, please let me know the reason, so that I can address the issue in future editions.

Historical travel guides
New York
Jersey in 1921
Norwich in 1880
Doon the Watter
Liverpool in 1886
Nottingham in 1899
Bournemouth in 1914
Great Yarmouth in 1880
Victorian Walks in Surrey
The Way We Were: Bath
A Victorian Visit to Brighton
The Way We Were: Lincoln
A Victorian Visit to Hastings
A Victorian Visit to Falmouth
Newcastle upon Tyne in 1903
Victorian and Edwardian York
The Way We Were: Llandudno
A Victorian Visit to North Devon
The Way We Were: Manchester
A Victorian Guide to Birmingham
Leeds through the Magic Lantern

Walking Books
Victorian Edinburgh Walks
Victorian Rossendale Walks
More Victorian Rossendale Walks
Victorian Walks on the Isle of Wight (Book 1)
Victorian Walks on the Isle of Wight (Book 2)
Victorian Rossendale Walks: The End of an Era

Other historical topics
The YMCA in the First World War
Sarah Jane's Victorian Tour of Scotland
The River Tyne through the Magic Lantern
The 1907 Wrench Cinematograph Catalogue
Victorian Street Life through the Magic Lantern
The First World War through the Magic Lantern
Ballyclare May Fair through the Victorian Magic Lantern
The Story of Burnley's Trams through the Magic Lantern
The Franco-British 'White City' London Exhibition of 1908
The 1907 Wrench 'Optical and Science Lanterns' Catalogue
The CWS Crumpsall Biscuit Factory through the Magic Lantern
How They Built the Forth Railway Bridge: A Victorian Magic
Lantern Show

Historical photo albums (just photos)
The Way We Were: Suffolk
Norwich: The Way We Were
The Way We Were: Somerset
Fife through the Magic Lantern
York through the Magic Lantern
Rossendale: The Way We Were
The Way We Were: Cumberland
Burnley through the Magic Lantern
Oban to the Hebrides and St. Kilda
Tasmania through the Magic Lantern
Swaledale through the Magic Lantern
Llandudno through the Magic Lantern
Birmingham through the Magic Lantern
Penzance, Newlyn and the Isles of Scilly
Great Yarmouth through the Magic Lantern
Ancient Baalbec through the Magic Lantern
The Isle of Skye through the Magic Lantern
Ancient Palmyra through the Magic Lantern
The Kentish Coast from Whitstable to Hythe
New South Wales through the Magic Lantern
From Glasgow to Rothesay by Paddle Steamer
Victorian Childhood through the Magic Lantern
The Way We Were: Yorkshire Railway Stations
Southampton, Portsmouth and the Great Liners

Newcastle upon Tyne through the Magic Lantern
Egypt's Ancient Monuments through the Magic Lantern
The Way We Were: Birkenhead, Port Sunlight and the Wirral
Ancient Egypt, Baalbec and Palmyra through the Magic
Lantern

Printed in Great Britain
by Amazon